The Next Trump Savior

J Loving

DEDICATION

This book is written for all the Americans who have sacrificed time, money, and lives for our country. May these sacrifices never be forgotten.

CONTENTS

1 INAUGURATION DAY

Keaven began:

"It's January 22, 2025. Chief Justice Roberts, Vice President Dunning, Speaker Ryan, Senator Braxton, reverend clergy, members of my family and friends, and my fellow citizens:

We are faced with precarious times. Unemployment has reached its highest point since the Great Depression. Sadly, it is the direct result of an unfair tax system and hikes in minimum wages designed to help Americans. Instead, the indirect effect has been to damage Americans' job prospects.

While American workers can do a job, many times, at a higher level of quality than other nations' work forces, American businesses have had but one choice in response to labor costs spiraling out of control: outsource jobs or face bankruptcy.

Worse still, while Democrats continue to argue theirs is the only party who cares about minorities, the plight of minorities has worsened. As but one example, African-American males face rates of unemployment higher than ever before.

Who among us would say that race relations have improved? Hate crimes have risen exponentially. The irony of our hate crimes legislation is that African-Americans claiming to kill Caucasian-American based on race are outside its ambit whereas Caucasian-Americans who kill African-Americans based on race fall inside the ambit of increased jail time. Killing in the name of race is killing in the name of race. It is hatred all the same. This sentencing situation is but one example of many governmental policies that overemphasize race over results.

The country is now roughly 30 percent Caucasian-American, 30 percent African-American, 30 percent Latin-American, and 10 percent other in its racial demographics. It would seem to be the time to end programs based on race or instead emphasize means testing (economic status) over race itself. The more governmental programs that emphasize race means the more the American public does. Likewise, hatred based on race increases. We can fully understand the vicious cycle.

For foreign policy, 50 countries have nuclear weapons and the missile technology to reach the US. Our overreliance on a missile shield could prove to be mistaken. Electromagnetic attacks could render the shield inoperable, leaving us defenseless to an ICBM attack.

Meanwhile, our role in the world has diminished, resulting in a dire situation. The Syrian Civil War has mushroomed to what essentially is best described as a world war. Simultaneously, we are combating ISIS in more than just Iraq these days.

The Russians recently shot down another commercial airliner without any response. It is only the fourth that Russia has shot down in the last 40 years, far more than all the other countries on earth have shot down in their combined histories.

Russia has seized Belarus, the Baltic Republics, Ukraine, Turkmenistan, Uzbekistan, Azerbaijan, Georgia, Moldova, and on and on. Russia has essentially reclaimed all the Soviet Union's former satellites and begun exerting influence over its former Warsaw Pact 'allies.' Who is to doubt Russia's intent with 100,000 tanks ready to roll on the peripheries of Europe's Great Democracies?

China has recaptured Taiwan, a country we professed a willingness to defend, an agreement on which you now know we have reneged. Our standing in the world has never been lower. Former allies hate us. Enemies deem us too weak to live up to our obligations.

In the face of all these problems, again you may ask why I chose to run for President. Again, I remind you of what I said many days ago in a small town in Iowa as I announced my candidacy for the Republican nomination for President. I am but a humble man, knowing none of the graces of an Ivy League education. However, I have been instilled with an increasingly uncommon belief system, a belief system which made this country great once and can again make this country great.

There is no liberal. There is no conservative. There is no white. There is no black. There is but American, the only relevant classification.

We are one family. If one is deprived of rights, we all are deprived of rights. As I told you during my campaign, anybody who fails to believe in the equality of all Americans can vote for another party. I do not want them in my party.

What you may not realize is that you, America's citizens, are not responsible for the country's slide. Your government's leaders have failed you. They told you what you wanted to hear, blamed downfalls on you, and then took full credit for the rare positives.

I again say there is no left and no right. President George

Washington warned of the failings of political parties. They would engage in political battles not to improve the plight of citizens but instead to score political points. How prophetic was Washington? The time for petty battles is over. The American public expects a government to work for them, not against them.

The work begins with the tax system. It must be made fairer with reduced rates to allow Americans to have a choice of how to spend their income. They have the right to have enough money to purchase homes and invest in the economy. Such investment benefits us all.

Simultaneously, our military spending must be more effective, not to prepare for war, but to be at parity with those who seek to enslave others with their ideologies. The implicit threat is surrender or die. Peace can only occur through strength, being strong enough that no other nation even considers endangering our interests.

Real and lasting peace is my foreign policy goal. The elimination of nuclear weapons is a step in that process. Ending terrorism forevermore is also part of that process.

I would not have thrown my hat in the ring if I did not believe these objectives could be accomplished. I stood then and stand now for America because I refuse to watch America fail.

America is the last best hope for this world. If freedom fails here, the world is a much darker place. There is evil in this world without any doubt. Where there is evil, there must be good to counter it. When right, American is that good.

I believe in every American citizen. Working together, we can accomplish what the rest of the world says we cannot. We can change our lives for the better. A long journey begins with but one step, but it requires each one of us to take that step together.

Dr. Joseph Warren's 'Boston Massacre Oration' provides us with the guiding light: 'Our country is in danger but not to be despaired of . . . . Our enemies are numerous and powerful, but . . . Heaven and earth will aid the resolution. On you [rely] the fortunes of America. You are to decide the important questions on which rest the happiness and the liberty of millions yet unborn. Act worthy of yourselves.'

I intend to do so. God, forever bless America. Thank you."

2 HUMBLE BEGINNINGS

Keaven Deal was born in January 1978 in Ft. Hood, Texas. The country was in the midst of its worst times economically since the Great Depression and politically since World War II. Hyperinflation, energy shortages, declining international standing, terrorism, nuclear weapons, and Communism's spread dominated the news. Prisoners of war were still in Vietnam. Months later, kidnapped US embassy employees were still captives in Iran. President Jimmy Carter had been an utter failure, and a man named Ronald Reagan came to the rescue, elected to restore America.

The country wondered how a man better known for being the Gipper, an actor, could somehow save the US from its worst moments. Keaven grew up, knowing this man as what a President was supposed to be. To be born in the US among all the countries in the world was a blessing. To be born in the US under the leadership of Reagan was divine destiny.

Kyla, Keaven's mom, was educated at Liberty University and served as a youth pastor. She believed Keaven was a blessing from God, knew he would be special and important to his world, and chose his name to remind him and others that this country was and would always be "one nation under God." "Heaven" would be too presumptuous and even sacrilegious, but "Keaven" was just right.

Darren, Keaven's father, was a soldier. He believed in America with all his heart and soul. He was deployed to the Sinai in September 1980 as part of "Operation Bright Star," to work with Egyptian armed forces, an olive branch measure resulting from the Camp

David peace accords of 1979. President Reagan redeployed Darren's unit to the Sinai in 1982. In 1983, his father served in Grenada as part of a rescue of American college students there.

In general, President Carter had been reluctant to use the military for anything. He had reduced military spending to the point that Keaven's family could barely survive on the income. As such, Darren first dreamed during the Carter administration of qualifying for special forces. Higher pay and increased opportunities to get involved were the rewards. As evidence of the extra involvement, special forces soldiers had already fought Cuban-sponsored revolutionaries in El Salvador in 1981. Darren did not qualify right away but kept trying, a Deal trademark.

As Keaven turned six, Darren finally qualified. The family was soon moving to Tampa, Florida. Darren Deal was now stationed at SOCOM, MacDill Air Force Base. Kyla easily found work as a youth pastor.

Keaven had the blessing to learn at the feet of a master public speaker, Kyla. So long as the width and breadth of Texas was Kyla's gravitas and charisma. She could get transform lives anywhere.

Now in the special forces, Darren was involved in international interventions all the way from Lebanon to Honduras to Bolivia from peace-keeping to anti-Communist insurgency to anti-drug campaigns. In fact, in 1988 alone, Darren was deployed to Honduras as part of Operation Golden Pheasant to counter a Nicaraguan insurgency and to Panama as further protection for the Panama Canal Zone.

In 1989, Darren was part of the Andean Initiative War on Drugs in South America. He later served as part of the unit that repelled an Aquino government coup attempt in Luzon, Philippines. He next participated in Operation Just Cause in Panama. Indeed, Darren was part of the group to seize General Noriega.

In 1990, Keaven's father secured the US Embassy in Monrovia, Liberia. In 1991, Darren was the leading edge of the spear during the Gulf War. Even after the war, he protected Kurds in Northern Iraq on various missions in 1991.

3 FLORIDA DREAMS

While Darren was off on his deployments, Kyla was left trying to educate Keaven. Sure, Keaven attended public schools, but there was so much more to learn. Growing up in Florida, Keaven developed an interest in many pastimes. At an early age, he not only learned how to swim in Tampa Bay but also how to surf.

At the same time, though, Kyla educated him about an important history. Florida's proximity to Cuba naturally led to discussions about the Cuban Missile Crisis, the Bay of Pigs, the Mariel Boatlift, and current US policy on immigrants escaping Cuba.

Like most history lessons, Keaven dutifully listened but not did not quite understand. That fact remained true until he and his mother took a day trip to Key West. Keaven was only nine but could swim like a dolphin. Kyla dreamed of him winning an Olympic gold medal in swimming someday. Why should she not with all the time they spent at the beach?

Anyway, that day Keaven was swimming in the Straits of Florida for sure but also quite possibly in some senses the Caribbean Sea and the Atlantic Ocean. While trying mentally to replay his mother's history lessons on Cuba, he noticed on the horizon a self-constructed wooden boat with a motor attached to it.

The plucky "boat" was barely afloat. There were four individuals, a father, mother, son, and daughter, so much like his own family save for the extra child. They appeared to be on the last legs of a trip from Cuba. They evidently were seeking freedom in the last bastion of the free, the United States.

As the craft was nearly to shore, the boat started sinking. Keaven looked back toward Kyla. She saw the look in his eyes, a fire, a desire, so similar to Darren's look any time he talked about combat missions.

Still at a large depth between the bottom and the surface of the water, swimming was the only option for the Cuban family. The father allowed his daughter to climb on his back as he swam them to shore. The mother tried to swim her son to shore but began struggling undoubtedly due to exhaustion and malnutrition from the escape attempt.

Keaven was close enough to shore to return to the beach quickly where he grabbed a gigantic beach ball. He then began swimming with the beach ball toward the mother and son.

The father bearing his daughter to shore evidently did not notice his wife and son struggling. Keaven swam rapidly and soon reached the mother and son before they went under for possibly the final time.

He pulled her arms toward the beach ball, wrapping them around it for her to use it as a flotation device. Keaven then put the son on his back, beginning freestyle-swimming kicks to propel the group grabbing the beach ball to shore. With his daughter safe, the father had swum to help Keaven the rest of the way to the beach.

Kyla was in a state of shock during the entirety of this crisis. Some presence, almost as if it were God himself, had frozen her in her tracks. This presence reassured her that everything would be all right.

In the midst of a continual outpouring of "Muchas gracias's"

("Thank you very much's") emanating from the Cuban immigrants, Kyla rushed to give Keaven a hug. Kyla remarked, "Dad would be so proud of you. I'm proud of you. What you just did was miraculous."

Keaven responded, "I just did what anybody would do. I can swim well. It's just like the parable of the talents you taught me. Instead of burying my talent, I used it to help."

The Cuban son hugged him, saying "Eres un americano. Eres libertad." ("You're an American. You're freedom.")

Keaven replied, "I'll nickname you, Cuba Libre. ¿Está bien? (Is that all right?)."

Others rushed to aid. One told Keaven that he was a hero. He responded, "No, my dad's a hero. He serves our country in the military. Even though I don't get to see him much, he loves me and shows me that love by helping our country."

Another of the helpers, overcome by the bravery and charisma, said, "You'll be governor someday. I'll call the newspapers. They'll help make you famous for this rescue."

Keaven replied, "My mom's always taught me that, if you run for political office, instead of 100 percent of the people possibly liking you, you'll only have half at best. I don't want fame for just doing what I could."

Keaven had met his first immigrants and first Cubans, had saved his first lives, and had set the stage for what would follow in his life. He would help without expecting press or even thanks.

That night, Kyla gave Keaven a Bible and a copy of the Constitution. She told him, "You've earned these special things. Dad and I were waiting for the right moment to give them to you, me the Bible and Dad the Constitution. Somehow this moment seems appropriate. You're meant for great things, and these two will light your path."

4 LIFE NOW FOREVER CHANGED

Then a man named Will Colton, believing in humanitarian interventions, ordered a special forces mission in Somalia. This President, the first with no military service in his background, had no problem ordering others into combat.

Keaven's dad sent home a picture of his unit attached to a postcard from each new deployment. Keaven had a collection of them and used them as bookmarks for his Bible.

In October of 1993, the Battle of Mogadishu loomed on the horizon. Task Force Ranger was ordered to capture an armed leadership group, comprising two of self-proclaimed Somali President Mohamed Farrah Aidid's top subordinates, Omar Salad Elmi, foreign minister, and Mohamed Hassan Awale, top political adviser. Darren, the tip of the spear as part of special forces, was there.

Keaven kept waiting for a postcard from the latest deployment, hoping every day it would arrive. After school, he would listen for the mail truck. Keaven would race to the mail box the moment he heard the truck each day. However, the days passed without a postcard coming. Keaven prayed every night a common prayer: "Lord, please take care of my father. He's so important to me. I've spent so little time with him. I need him, so please return him home to me safely."

Kyla was worried, too. However, she was used to the secrecy of special forces. Sometimes communications could not occur for days because of confidential operations. At times, the postcards came long after Darren's unit was already out of the deployment area.

News started breaking about the Battle of Mogadishu. As Kyla heard about the special forces' involvement, her fear grew. As she heard of the casualties and the descriptions of how dire the situation was, that fear increased exponentially.

As Keaven arrived home from school two days later, there was a military Humvee parked in the drive. Two soldiers were standing next to it. Keaven somehow remembered them from his father's pictures. One soldier had his arm in a sling. The other had crutches. Both seemed to have combat-related injuries. Kyla told Keaven, "Get out of the car and lock yourself in your bedroom right away."

Keaven knew how to follow orders, unlocking the front door with his mother's key and racing to his bedroom. Kyla followed him in, inviting the soldiers into the living room. She, too, seemed to know who they were.

Keaven generally followed orders, but something stopped him from doing so this day. He opened his bedroom door a crack not only to be able to hear but also to watch the conversation take place. In seconds, his life changed forever. He heard: "hero," "saved our lives," "Battle of Mogadishu," and then "killed in action." Simultaneously, his mother collapsed. The soldier with the arm in a sling helped her up, saying "I'd better take her to the emergency room just to ensure she's okay. Can you stay with the kid?"

The other soldier, with crutches, answered, "Sure."

Keaven started crying. He knew what the words meant. He rushed to his mom, but the soldier with the arm in a sling nudged him aside. The soldier with crutches said, "Did your Dad ever teach you to follow orders?'

Keaven responded with tears flowing, "Yes, sir."

The soldier continued, "Your orders are to sit on your couch with me while your mom gets medical attention. You need to know about your father."

The two were alone in the room. The soldier remarked, "I'm Matt, part of your father's special forces unit." He shook Keaven's hand.

Matt continued, "I served with your father a long time. He'd share the letters you and your mother wrote to him. We all wished we had a family waiting for us at home just like he did."

"You may not realize it, but the words you wrote to him were so powerful that they inspired each one of us," Matt stated. "A lot of times, we would wonder if anybody really understood or cared about what we went through," Matt opined.

He continued, "They're always protestors somewhere as we return. We had an easier time ignoring them after you wrote him a note, saying: 'If you or your brothers are ever scared, hungry, tired, or hurting, know that I'm praying for you with all that I have so that there's no way God or Uncle Sam will ever forget to take care of you.' What powerful words, Keaven."

Matt started to cry. Keaven stopped crying for the moment and hugged Matt. It did not stop Matt from crying. Matt responded, "We'd do anything to bring your father back. He saved our lives. There isn't a one of us who wouldn't have died in his place so that he could live."

Matt reached for his pocket, taking out the postcard picture of the unit that Darren could not send. He also took out Darren's dog tag.

Trying to stave off his tears, Matt commanded, "We all have an obligation to ensure Darren's sacrifice was not in vain and that his memory will carry on." He then handed the two items to Keaven, saying, "If you ever need help, let us know. Every soldier in the unit is committed to helping you and Kyla in any way possible so long as we live."

The other soldier returned without Kyla, speaking in Matt's ear. Suddenly, Matt asked Keaven, "Are you still able to follow orders?"

Keaven replied, "Yes, sir."

Matt said, "We're taking you to the hospital to see your mom." The whole way there, Keaven kept hearing: "so unfair."

At the hospital, Keaven ran to his mother's side, hugging her. Kyla spoke with tears in her own eyes, "You're going to have to be strong for Dad in Heaven and for me. There's a reason that I passed out. The doctors told me I have cancer. It spread from my breast to the rest of my body. During the Carter administration's military cuts, our poverty, I developed the habit of not having medical check-ups. That part doesn't matter. What matters is that they've not giving me long to live."

Keaven had cried so much that day already that he almost did not have any tears left. He buried his head in the covers next to his mother's side, asking rhetorically, "Where's God?"

5 ARLINGTON CEMETERY

Terence and Matt drove Keaven to Arlington for Darren's burial. Kyla was not allowed to travel. On the way, the two soldiers told Keaven more about his father's heroics. Somali militia and armed civilians shot down Darren's Black Hawk helicopter. That act did not stop him. Darren fought off hundreds or thousands of armed Somalis long enough to allow his comrades to be rescued. In the process, though, he was killed on the verge of being rescued himself. 18 Americans were killed. It was the bloodiest battle since Vietnam, a war in which the President had somehow found a way to avert serving.

On this day meant to honor soldiers killed in Mogadishu, Keaven saw the rows and rows of crosses and stars of David. He witnessed the eternal flame. A bugler played taps. Rifles were fired as part of an honor guard. Fighters flew overhead in missing-man formation.

President Colton personally handed Darren's Medal of Honor and an American flag to Keaven, smiling long enough for the cameras to capture the moment. President Colton was always aware of the cameras.

Keaven wanted to say something, anything, to the President from "Why did you order the action?" to "Why are you taking advantage of me now with all the media present?" to "Why are you retreating after these sacrifices?" Keaven felt an anger building in him, knowing that these pictures of the momentarily saintly President looking out for a child of the fallen would improve the President's dismal ratings.

Indeed, his ratings had nowhere to go but up after this alleged failure. The press said the mission was a failure. US forces were withdrawn before capturing Aidid and securing a peace, so failure seemed to be the proper adjective.

To avert future bad press assessments, President Colton cancelled all military actions against Aidid and sought peace by appointing a special envoy to Somalia. The President then assured that all US forces would be withdrawn by March 31, 1994.

To avert bad press contemporaneously then, the President made sure the blame fell directly on Commander Garrison and the Secretary of Defense. Of course, the buck could never stop where it was supposed to stop despite what Harry Truman used to say.

Those ill-advised Presidential decisions laid the groundwork for 9/11. Osama bin Laden viewed the withdrawal as evidence of US weakness. It renewed his wavering confidence that he could defeat the US and doubled his resolve to strike, 9/11.

The alleged failure in Mogadishu stopped President Colton from future interventions. The Rwandan Genocide of 1994 went on without any US intervention at all.

While Keaven was at Arlington Cemetery, his mom passed away. Keaven never had another chance to tell either parent how much he loved them. The God to whom Keaven prayed every night to take care of his family seemed not to care or, worse still, not to exist.

Terence was back on active duty. Matt was reassigned to another base and another unit. Keaven was essentially alone. That situation quickly ended. A case worker from Florida's social services had come to see him, telling him that he was too young to live alone and that his uncle was adopting him. Keaven responded, "My dad didn't have any brothers."

The social worker corrected him, indicating, "Yes, he did. Maybe he never spoke of him for some reason or another, but you definitely have an uncle. What's more is he wants to adopt you. It's a wonderful act of kindness."

Keaven winced at the words "wonderful act of kindness." Seeing the revulsion in Keaven's face, the social worker replied, "You could have been trapped in the foster care system. You would have been shuffled around to unrelated fosters until permanent placement could be found. You're the lucky one."

Keaven obviously did not feel lucky. He was hurting. The God he believed in was seemingly absent as his family, all that he had to love in this world, was taken away from him. An uncle, somehow related, was supposed to replace the most caring, giving parents in the history of the world.

The social worker continued, "You don't seem to realize how lucky you are. He's Davide Weiner, a Democratic Congressman from a Los Angeles, California, suburb. He already has two adopted kids. The first is an African-American 18-year-old high school senior from Compton, who's lived with him for the last four years. The other is a Latin-American 16-year-old high school junior, a former undocumented alien whose parents died in the process of illegally entering the US, who's lived with him for the last two years."

Keaven intoned, "First of all, a person is a person, not a hyphenated adjective. Their respective races are unimportant.

Second, there seems to be a pattern. Doesn't there?"

The social worker seemed not to understand, saying, "What do you mean?"

"Every two years that he's up for election, he seems to adopt somebody," Keaven answered. "That pattern indicates a lack of interest in the child's welfare but a great interest in getting re-elected, which makes the adoption seem pointless from my perspective," Keaven continued.

The social worker had a strange look on her face and replied, "All your teachers say that you're a model student and cause no problems. You can't be that cynical. Can you?"

Keaven, barely a teenager then, had no patience for her response, "Aren't you the person supposed to be looking out for my best interests? Did you ever think to ask him how somebody with the last name of Weiner is related to somebody with the last name of Deal?"

The social worker replied, "He was a stepbrother of your father's."

Keaven continued, "So I have no choice in the matter?"

She replied, "No, get packed because I'm taking you to the airport. The Congressman has agreed to pay for the ticket."

Keaven sarcastically replied, "How kind of him." Keaven began packing his mother's suitcase that was now his. He carefully placed the Bible with the postcards, a dog tag, the Constitution, his clothes, the flag, and the Medal of Honor in it.

The social worker continued, "Don't worry about your parent's belongings. The Congressman has agreed to take care of their estate by serving as executor. He'll act as a trustee of what they had until you're 18."

Keaven ironically intoned, "Don't worry. President Carter made sure that we don't have anything. In fact, I'm sure that, being a Democrat, Davide will find a way to make sure the government gets whatever is left."

"You, Republicans," the social worker replied, sighing.

Keaven replied, "I'm not a Republican or a Democrat. I can't vote until I'm 18, so there's no way I can be registered as either."

The social worker explained, "I don't care. I get tired of dealing with that attitude of being able to take care of yourself without government help. Look at this situation. If you didn't have me, you may never have connected with your Democratic uncle."

Keaven responded, "Thank you." Keaven stopped for a moment to view his home for the last time, considering that his life with his parents could end up being the only happy moments he would experience in his life.

"Come on," she said. "The government doesn't pay me to look out for spoiled kids like you. My time's better spent on really needy kids who deserve my help."

6 LEFTIST COAST

There to meet him at the Los Angeles International Airport were his two new stepbrothers, Raul and Jessie, his new stepmom, Orchard, and a combination butler and driver, Frankie. Keaven knew he was never going to fit in. Everybody greeting him was wearing the most in-style clothes, expensive clothes. He was wearing but a plain white t-shirt, lugging a decades-old, worn-out suitcase.

Orchard greeted him by pretending to kiss each of his cheeks, the faux French greeting that it was. She said, "How precious you are. I love this moment, greeting the new kid." Orchard then told Frankie, "Throw his suitcase away and its contents."

She returned her attention to Keaven, saying, "We get to go shopping in Beverly Hills because no actress's kid is going to look like white trash." She continued, "It would ruin my image."

In the series of exchanges, Keaven began to grab his suitcase more tightly than ever before. As Frankie made a move toward it, Keaven said, "I'll put it in the trunk for you, Frankie."

Orchard intervened, "You shouldn't be so mean to the hired help."

Raul then grabbed Keaven's hand in a handshake designed to squeeze all the blood out of it, saying, "Hola, hermano ("Hello, brother)." Keaven did not back down, grabbing back with all his might, saying, "Encantado, hermano" ("Enchanted to meet you, brother"). Kyla had obviously taught Keaven Spanish, a second language of helpful use in Florida.

Jessie was next, offering a high five but pulling his hand away just before the high five could be executed. He said, "Too slow, man."

Keaven grabbed Jessie's arm, raised it in the air, and then completed the high five, saying, "Everybody who underestimates me tends to be disappointed in the end, even for something as insignificant as a high five." Keaven shot him a menacing glance.

Orchard intervened, "Come on, family. There could be reporters or cameras around, so we have to look the part of a family."

Keaven interrupted, "Don't worry. It's good to know that we're here based on form, not substance."

Jessie commanded, "Are you making a racist comment because that comment sounded racist?"

Keaven replied, "Don't worry, older brother. I'll make sure you know if I'm insulting you."

Soon the press did arrive as it became apparent that Orchard had planned for exactly that outcome. If it furthered her movie career and secondarily Davide's re-election campaign, she was all for it. Orchard put her arm around Keaven, whispering in his ear, "Smile, or I'll kill you."

Keaven's only thought was, "I guess this is why they say Hollywood is killing our culture."

As they arrived at Keaven's new home with bags of new clothes, Keaven noticed the fleet of sports cars in the driveway and the mansion in the background. Keaven had lived in small homes his entire life, the plight of soldiers' families. This Democratic Congressman, who had championed cutting military funding for so many years, did not have any problem finding money for himself.

In fact, as Frankie opened the door to the mansion, Keaven noticed that Davide was in the midst of asking Hollywood directors, producers, actors, and actresses for campaign donations. Thankfully, Keaven was still carrying his suitcase, now especially to the dismay of Orchard, who was always bent on form over substance. She quietly told Frankie to lead the kids up the stairs. However, she was not quick enough.

Davide walked the assembled crowd of celebrities over toward Keaven, introducing him as the newest member of his family. In fact, he explained, "I rescued Jessie from Compton, South Central LA. I saved Raul from a life of poverty as an undocumented orphaned child. Now I have saved Keaven, the son of a deceased military hero and a cancer victim. He'll complete my demographics, meaning any right-leaning liberal will vote for me now. We all know of course there are no Republicans in this district."

Davide, Orchard, Jessie, Raul, and the assembled crowd all begin laughing. "How funny" Keaven thought to himself. He was in the exact situation he expected from the start.

Davide then motioned for Frankie to walk them away. Orchard wanted to make sure to get her face in the midst of so many stars and star-makers to benefit her career. Before Keaven was relegated to his room, though, he wanted to make a great first impression, "Isn't it amazing how easy it is to get along with enough money around? Someday, I'll take you all to the real world, a military base, where soldiers' families live in humble homes while their beloved risk their lives and die to allow you to be free."

A famous Hollywood celebrity responded, "Only ignorant men and women fight in wars."

Before Keaven could respond, Orchard shoved her hand over his mouth. She quickly walked him to his room. Keaven was surprised somebody so thin could be that strong. He resolved to start lifting weights if any were around.

Davide tried to allay the guests by saying, "I apologize for him. He's from the South. You obviously understand the significant re-education he'll require to move on from being raised in a redneck household. What a shame it is that the South spends so little money on education, which is why education should be federally administered."

Keaven considered biting Orchard's hand just to be able to say something in response but thought the better of it. Keaven had never considered whether he was a Republican or Democrat. He had been taught to do what was right, meaning that the right decisions for this country did not relate to what party doctrine was but instead to what helped Americans. However, the Leftist Coast evidently had different answers to such questions.

Finally in his spacious new bedroom, Orchard read him the riot act. She began, "You have the good fortune to have access to the best of the best Hollywood has to offer. Act thankful. I had to crawl through hell to get the career that I've had. I would've died to have the opportunity you have, being young and famous in the midst of Hollywood."

Keaven replied, "You may remember that my parents just died, meaning that I am supposed to, as a kid, be going through a lengthy period of recovery and adjustment."

Orchard replied, "I've been through two drug rehabs, so don't tell me about recovery." She then left the room.

Soon Jessie and Raul had entered Keaven's room. Jessie began the initiation, saying, "We lucked out being saved from poverty, getting to this situation. We're not about to let you ruin that."

Raul continued, "We have to do what we're told to get Davide re-elected. Our standing in school relies on it. Everybody else is connected to Hollywood. I mean a kid who's related to an actor or actress out of favor gets relegated. Imagine what would happen to us if Davide did not get re-elected."

Jessie interrupted, "With him in office, we're like gods. Any girl in school. Well, any woman in this area will do whatever you want because you're the kid of somebody famous."

Keaven responded, "I'm not his kid."

Raul intervened, "They don't know and don't care. He's important, so everybody wants to get in your good graces to make themselves important by proxy. Their parents even tell them to get tight with us to further their standing."

Jessie pulled out his wallet, revealing countless pictures of beautiful women. He continued, "Again, we're talking celebrities, older than teenagers, are interested in us. How can you not be thankful?"

Keaven replied, "Sow to the flesh. Reap to the flesh."

Raul countered, "That religious stuff doesn't work here. A

Democratic Congressman from Hollywood doesn't believe in God, so his kids don't either."

Keaven continued, "I'm only 15, guys."

Jessie responded, "So? I was sleeping with girls at age 15."

Keaven replied, "Stop joking."

Jessie countered, "I'm not joking."

"What were you thinking?" Keaven questioned.

Raul answered, "This is Hollywood. This isn't some backward Southern state."

Jessie emphasized, "We've been through hell in our lives, and we're not going back. Live by our rules, or . . . ."

Keaven countered, "Or what? Are you going to kill me like Orchard said she was?"

Raul mentioned, "Davide, Orchard, and their crew may be anti-violence, but we're not."

Jessie expanded, "In fact, if we took you out, we could always say it was self-defense against a white supremacist. The courts in LA will believe us over you most importantly because you wouldn't be around to defend yourself."

Keaven responded, "I don't care how much bigger you are, big brothers. I'm not scared of anything."

Jessie grabbed Keaven's suitcase and then started to dig through it. He grabbed the Bible, the Constitution, the Medal of Honor, the flag, the dog tag, and the postcards. Jessie said, "Each time you disobey us, we'll burn one of these items. He took out a lighter and lit the Constitution on fire. He threw it in the room's trashcan, saying,

"Any document that says African-Americans don't deserve a full vote is the first to go."

Raul held Keaven down so that he could not intervene. Keaven fought with all his might but could not overcome his bigger, older brother's strength. Raul mentioned, "While you're at it, burn the Bible. It'll just be trouble for us if he still has it."

Keaven tried to yell, but Raul was crafty and had already stuffed his mouth with a blanket. Again, Keaven tried to fight off his older brother but could not. Jessie burned the Bible as well. This time, he did not hesitate to laugh, causing Raul to start laughing.

Keaven did not want to show his hurt, but he could not help but cry. The Bible and the Constitution were from his dad and mom, some of the last possessions he had from them.

Jessie looked at the Medal of Honor, the flag, the dog tag, and the postcards and then said, "I'll lock these items up. If you play by the rules, I won't burn them or throw them in the garbage. If you don't, well, it's your choice. Enjoy California."

They laughed as they started to exit the room. Keaven tried to rifle through the trashcan to save the Bible and the Constitution but to no avail. As they were walking out the door, Keaven dried the tears from his eyes. He then stated, "You can take away all my possessions, but you can't take away my mind. You may place me in bondage, but you can't enslave my spirit. Every time you hurt me, you make me stronger. Every time you take from me, you make me more determined. I'm right. Therefore, I have might, and, in the end, I will prevail."

Jessie replied, "We have no problem knocking those memories from your mind."

The only problem for Jessie and Raul was now, with the door open, everybody could hear what was being said. Orchard grabbed Jessie by the ear and pulled him to his room. Again, Keaven was left thinking, "How could somebody so thin be so strong?" Raul evidently was used to this routine and left before she could come back to grab him by his ear, too.

Orchard returned, saying to Keaven behind a close door, "What's with the smoke? Were you using drugs?"

"No, I don't believe in drugs," Keaven responded. "They cloud the mind, which could be the problem for Jessie and Raul given they just decided to burn my Bible and Constitution."

Orchard commanded, "It's all for the better. There's no time or place for either here in LA. There is no morality at all. Good night."

Keaven knew how to follow orders. However, Orchard was not in his chain of command. He snuck out of his room and did recon on the house. He discovered in fact that there was a weight room. He resolved to spend every spare moment there to ensure he would never be pushed around again. Before the recon ended, Keaven snuck into Jessie's room and recaptured his remaining possessions: the Medal of Honor, the flag, the dog tag, and the postcards.

As he returned to his bedroom from this recon, Keaven considered how difficult his life had become. His faith was in a rough spot, which could only worsen in the immorality capital of the world. Tomorrow would be his first day of class in a new school. Keaven knew better than to stereotype any group of individuals. However, his first experiences with Californians had left him wanting for more.

Keaven considered the concept of hate for a moment. He wanted to hate his new family. However, Keaven had experienced so much love that he could not feel hate even in this moment. For the time being, he was not going to return to prayer. He regretted the fact that Orchard would win on that point, but it ultimately was his hurt, not hate, that led to this choice.

7 BEVERLY HILLS HIGH SCHOOL

Frankie prepared breakfast for Jessie, Raul, and Keaven. Davide and Orchard evidently were not morning types. Frankie handed them each a $20 bill. Keaven replied, "What's this? Is it our allowance for the month?"

Jessie and Raul laughed. Frankie replied, "It's your lunch money."

Keaven questioned, "Why don't we get meal tickets for lunch at school?"

Raul responded, "There is no way there could be just a regular school lunch."

Jessie intoned, "There are vegetarians, practicing Jews who only accept kosher products, and . . . ."

Raul interrupted, "There are so many different groups that it would be a waste of food to serve one common meal. It wouldn't fit some group, and they'd end up throwing it away."

Jessie corrected, "The food's never wasted. They'd find some environmentally friendly way of using it."

Raul replied, "See how easy it is to get along with us. Your life will be a dream. We'll show you the ropes."

Jessie continued, "I mean the sun is already shining. It's going to be 70 degrees today without any precipitation like it is every day. This is freakin' Heaven."

"Think of the best looking chicas you've ever seen in your life and then multiply it by ten," Raul continued.

Jessie countered, "No multiply by 100. The girls here are unbelievable, and you have the threads that are in vogue. You have the connections and the clothes, and every girl will be all over you."

Raul intervened, "We'll show you the ropes today. Meet us for lunch. Enjoy your classes. The teachers are all about making you feel good about yourself, so they try not to grade anything. If they did, you might feel bad about yourself."

Keaven questioned, "How much do you learn, though, in that environment?"

"Who cares?" Jessie countered. "Beverly Hills is about enjoying yourself."

Jessie and Raul exchanged high fives. Keaven countered, "How will you be ready for college, though?"

Raul responded, "With the money and connections the Congressman has, we'll always be provided for. College is for the unconnected and the poor."

Frankie led them to a limousine to drive them to school. Keaven said, "You can't be serious."

Jessie replied, "I know. I ask the Congressman every day for my own wheels to drive to school, a sports car, a Ferrari. He hasn't relented."

Raul continued, "Yet."

Jessie went on, saying, "He'll give in someday, especially if he's re-elected. Then I may be willing to give you two a ride once every so often."

All Keaven could do was shake his head. He thought of all the military families and their suffering in humble housing and then of how a Congressman who had defunded them could live the lifestyle he did.

Just before they arrived at school, Jessie mentioned, "Don't worry. Davide will be returning to the Capitol soon. Then we'll be back to hosting parties, and you'll see how wild . . . ."

Raul interrupted, finishing the sentence, "how wonderful it can get."

Jessie continued, "Get your Ray-Bans on."

Keaven replied, "I didn't bring sunglasses."

Raul countered, "They're not sunglasses. They're Ray-Bans, and you can borrow my second pair. Just get them back to me safely."

Keaven responded, "How wonderful."

They disembarked from the limousine into what can best be described as La-La Land. Keaven had never dated a girl, but he had no problem agreeing with his brothers' descriptions. The problem was that Keaven believed in so much more than outer appearance. He would have to ascertain whether all that glittered was really gold or instead pyrite. That process meant finding out what was really in the souls of all these individuals.

Keaven had a gift. He seemed to be able to figure out who needed help on the turn of a dime. Until the first bell, all the students were gathered around the outside of the school. Keaven noticed a girl sitting by herself and asked Raul who she was. Raul responded, "That's Rosa. She's an undocumented alien. Her family was recently deported, but somehow she was not caught."

Jessie countered, "She's now living with the biggest playboy in Hollywood. Lucky girl."

Keaven replied, "Is that a healthy environment? What about her foster mom?"

Raul answered, "She just has a foster dad."

Keaven questioned, "Isn't her social services worker concerned about that environment?"

Raul countered, "If the choice is between living in a border town in poverty or living with a rich American, every Mexican would choose the latter."

Keaven continued, "I don't mean what she would choose from the outside looking in. I mean that somebody else has to be looking out for her to get her out of a potentially bad situation."

Jessie countered, "This is Hollywood. Celebrities get what they want. The government doesn't interfere with celebrities. They're the ones bringing in the money that helps pay the government's bills."

Keaven asked, "How much English does she speak?"

Raul commanded, "She knows both English and Spanish. I know what you're thinking. She looks hot and everything. You can do better."

Jessie continued, "In fact, you would make us look bad if you choose for one of your girlfriends somebody that low in the social order here."

Keaven asked, "One of your girlfriends?"

Raul countered, "The more popular you are, the more girlfriends you have."

Jessie intervened, "And we're really popular."

Keaven replied, "I'm not looking for a girlfriend. I'm looking to help somebody who just happens to be a girl and who looks like she could use a friend."

Raul mentioned, "You don't have to hide behind words. Just say what you really want. LA is not about hiding behind words. You say what you want, and you get it."

Yet again, all Keaven could do was shake his head.

Pointing to somebody else, Jessie mentioned, "How about that girl? Neither of us is interested in her, but her father runs a movie studio."

Raul cajoled, "It would help our standing."

Keaven answered, "Thanks, but no thanks." He began walking toward Rosa.

Jessie told Raul, "What a lost cause."

Raul replied, "We thought by getting a Caucasian-American brother we would improve our standing."

Jessie countered, "Oh, well. We'll just have to live on four girlfriends each."

"Speak for yourself, Jessie," Raul countered. "I'm working on my sixth."

Raul and Jessie again slapped high fives.

Reaching Rosa, Keaven said, "Hello, Rosa. Is it, Rosa? I'm Keaven."

Rosa replied, "Please don't bother me. I don't feel like talking."

Keaven continued, "One of my flaws is that I'm pretty good about noticing somebody who looks like they may need help."

Rosa countered sarcastically, "Obviously I don't need help

because I'm just so lucky to live with the most wonderful of Hollywood celebrities."

Keaven intervened, saying, "Lo entiendo. Todas las personas en mi familia están en el cielo ahora. Al menos, tu familia está viva." (I understand. All the people in my family are in Heaven now. At least your family is alive.")

Rosa replied, "How is it that somebody who is white (I mean Caucasian-American) knows how to speak Spanish?"

Keaven responded, "Don't they teach Spanish as a foreign language here?"

Smiling, Rosa countered, "Keaven, they only speak Valley even though they try to teach them Spanish as a second language in school."

Keaven replied, "It's nice to see you smile. You have a beautiful smile."

Rosa calmly stated, "You should find a better friend. I'm not looking to date anybody. I am at best damaged goods."

Keaven asked, "What do you mean?"

The first bell rang. Rosa countered, "Saved by the bell. It's obvious you are new. Here is some advice to survive from somebody who knows. Get with the right crowd. Life is survivable then."

Keaven started to make his way to the first class on his schedule. He carefully considered what Rosa had just told him.

8 LUNCH TOGETHER

At lunch, Keaven saw the prices on the food and just could not commit to buying anything. The prices were outrageous. He set down his empty tray and tried to look for a place to sit. Jessie was surrounded by his four girlfriends, and Raul was in the midst of his six.

Keaven thought to himself, "Why would any girl want to be part of a harem for either?" They certainly did not like Jessie or Raul for their personalities. Keaven had never met anybody so shallow. The girls did not act like real girlfriends either. They were just around them to soak up the popularity that emanated from them due to their connection to a Congressman.

As it never seemed to rain in California, the cafeteria was outdoors. Rosa was sitting on the ground next to a fence alone again. She was not eating anything either. Keaven sat down next to her.

Keaven said, "I never would have guessed you'd be in the same classes as I am."

Rosa replied, "Just to let you know, I'm 15."

Keaven answered, "I'm 15, too, so we were meant to hang together. Why are you not eating?"

Rosa countered, "Why are you not eating?"

"I asked first," Keaven replied with a smile.

"I asked better," Rosa countered with a laugh.

"I can't stand to waste money on food that expensive," Keaven replied. "My family lived in virtual poverty, spending far less on food meant for an entire day for an entire family than this lunch would cost."

Rosa replied, "Been there. Done that. I'm not eating today because my foster dad says I have to lose weight."

Keaven laughed. "You're joking. Right?"

Rosa looked sadly back, saying, "No joke. He's used to hanging out with models who starve themselves, heroin addicts even."

Keaven countered, "You're thinner than a rail. Besides, what matters is on the inside, not the outside."

Rosa laughed, saying, "What a joke. This is LA. Everything is about the outside. Inside counts for nothing. How can you be so naïve?"

Keaven countered, "Everybody tells me it's because I'm from the South."

With a wry smile, Rosa replied, "Obviously I'm from the South, too, Mexico."

"Mira (Look): I can tell you have a beautiful soul, but it's troubled," Keaven intoned.

"You don't even know about LA, so how would you know?" Rosa questioned. "Even if you knew, how could you ever help me? Besides, what would be in it for you?"

"I once saved the life of a Cuban immigrant and didn't do it for anything," Keaven replied.

Rosa continued, "Every American guy I've ever met has always wanted something. No good turn is ever free."

Before Keaven could reply, Jessie and Raul were pulling him over to their table. Jessie reminded Keaven, "I told you to meet with us at lunch."

Raul scolded, "I might have already lost a girlfriend because of you associating with somebody so low in the social order."

Keaven intervened, "I would have sat with you if there were a seat available. I mean some of the girls were literally sitting on your laps. As if there were enough room for me to sit next to you."

Keaven motioned for Rosa to follow. Raul countered, "Only Keaven's invited. Have fun sitting next to the fence, Rosa."

Rosa looked away. Keaven noticed a tear coming to her eye.

Keaven tried to break away, saying, "Raul, you're pretty cruel."

Jessie interjected, "Cruelty describes what you are doing to our social standing already on your first day here. Remember the deal about playing by the rules, our rules?"

Keaven replied, "I get it, guys."

Jessie then motioned to two girls, saying, "French. Toast. Come here."

Keaven asked, "You have to be kidding me."

Raul said, "I know. You can thank us later."

Keaven replied, "No, I mean somebody actually named twins, French and Toast?"

Jessie mentioned, "Remember that actors and actresses are artists. An inventive name for a kid is artistic."

Raul continued, "An inventive name gets more press, too, meaning the parents get renewed interest in work."

Jessie countered, "You can thank us later for introducing you to the most surgically augmented girls in school, who just so happen to be twins."

Keaven replied, "So how beautiful are their souls if you know so much about them?"

Raul countered, "You're always a kidder."

Keaven was left shaking his head once again. This time, though, the reaction at least allowed him glances at Rosa. He felt terrible about how she had been treated. Keaven resolved that he was going to make up for it after school. While he may have been from the South, somehow a disability on the Leftist Coast, he felt like he had a better understanding of Rosa's true situation than anybody else. Keaven was not about to let her continue to suffer.

Keaven was lucky enough to be in Rosa's last class for the day, making his resolved course of action even easier. Keaven walked out of school with Rosa toward her foster dad. Rosa told Keaven, "You can't be seen with me."

Instead of running away, Keaven stood in front of her and would not move. It blocked her path to her foster dad and his waiting Ferrari. Rosa continued, "What are you doing? You don't understand how much trouble you'll get me in."

Keaven replied, "You're coming home with me tonight. I know what's going on."

Rosa sternly countered, "You don't understand. You'll get me in more trouble than I'm in."

Keaven answered, "I fully understand. I saw the bruises on your arms. You're not ever going back with him again."

Rosa tried desperately to walk around him, but Keaven would not move. Rosa pleaded, "You have to move. If you don't move, they won't help me get my family back to the US."

Keaven questioned, "Is that what he's been promising in exchange for your silence?"

Rosa countered, "What silence?"

Frankie pulled up with the limousine. Keaven then turned to Rosa's foster dad, saying, "I invited Rosa to sleep over at Congressman Weiner's house tonight in her own room. She accepted."

Rosa tried to yell, "No, I didn't.

Keaven found strength he did not know he had to pull Rosa to the waiting limousine.

Jessie tried to intervene. Keaven stopped him, saying, "I don't want to hear it. She's going to be safe with us for at least tonight."

Raul questioned, "But our social status?"

Keaven replied, "I'm going to teach you about substance over form."

Frankie interrupted, "Orchard doesn't want me to bring anybody else home."

Mastering the most powerful voice he could, Keaven replied, "A human's well-being comes before an orchard's."

"Raul and Jessie, meet Rosa," Keaven continued. "She's a person, not a social status."

Jessie again tried to interject. Keaven stopped him, saying, "She's also being abused, possibly worse than just bruises."

Raul countered, "I thought we taught you about playing by the rules. What Orchard says is to be followed, or we risk losing this Heaven."

Keaven replied, "You wouldn't know what Heaven is if it hit you in the face."

Rosa intervened, "The chances of my family getting back to the US will be zero if you don't get me back to my foster dad."

Jessie interjected, "You see. She doesn't even want our help. We're not even allowed to bring girls back or even guys, so why do you think you can?"

Raul mentioned, "She's not worth it. You can get a million more of her right at the border."

"You should know because you're the same as me," Rosa countered.

Raul replied, "No, I'm better than you are."

Frankie intoned, "We're all going to get in trouble for this. Can't we just drop her off somewhere else?"

Keaven asked, "If you had Jesus Christ in the car and his accusers were pursuing him to put him on the cross, would you look away? Would you give him up?"

Jessie commented, "She's no Jesus Christ. She's slept with her foster dad."

Keaven replied, "So you knew yet did nothing and said nothing."

Raul intervened, "Everybody knows. Celebrities get what they want. There are no rules that apply to them. Why do you think she's in the lowest social class? Nobody wants to be around her because of the STDs that her foster dad's probably given her." Rosa slapped him in the face. They were home.

Keaven commanded, "It's time to work as a team. Frankie, you distract Orchard by bringing her in the kitchen and explaining that you should be allowed to get a new food processor. Jessie, you grab Davide and ask him to talk in the backyard about how you can help him win more of the minority vote in the coming election. Raul, we'll give each 60 seconds to get their marks in position. Then you'll walk in front of Rosa with me behind her. If Davide or Orchard break contact with Frankie or Jessie, we'll have to act as a blanket of humanity to hide Rosa. We'll bring her to my room. I'll sleep on the couch tonight."

Frankie ironically replied, "Great plan, General, except they have guests coming over tonight in minutes, and they'll be on guard for anything suspicious because of how important the event is."

Keaven replied, "The plan will work. Trust me." Surely enough, Rosa and Keaven were secreted away in his bedroom. Somehow, everybody followed the plan to the letter. Of course, it helped that they knew the consequences of being caught would be obliteration at the hands of Orchard.

Keaven said to Rosa, "You don't ever have to worry about being abused again. Congressman Weiner is a Democrat. Democrats are supposed to be the most in favor of protecting women from abuse. He has to help you, Rosa. Because of Democrats' belief in helping immigrants, he may well help your parents return to America, too."

Rosa replied, "Why are you doing this for me? What do you really want?"

Keaven sighed, saying, "Is this what LA teaches us? Nobody does anything just because it is the right thing to do. It only gets done if it personally serves your interests."

Rosa kissed Keaven. Keaven replied, "You didn't have to kiss me."

Rosa replied, "I wanted to. Whether it's my nationality, race, foster dad, whatever, nobody has ever treated me as well as you have. I've known you but one day, yet you are doing more for me than anybody else in America ever has."

Keaven responded, "By the way, your English is better than mine."

The door suddenly opened. Standing there were Davide, Orchard, and unfortunately Rosa's foster dad. Davide grabbed Rosa by the arm and led her back toward her foster dad, saying, "See. She's safe and sound, ready for your caring embrace again."

Keaven intervened, "That man is abusing her. You can't let her return with him. She won't be safe."

Davide countered, "This man is not abusing her. He's a major supporter of my re-election campaign."

Keaven stood in front of his new stepdad, saying, "I won't get out of the way."

Orchard grabbed Keaven, pulling him out of the way.

Keaven implored his new stepparents, "She is an underage girl being physically and emotionally abused. She needs your help. If you don't tell the police, I'll tell them myself."

Davide reassured Rosa's foster dad, "Don't worry. The chief of police is here tonight, and he's on my side. That means he's on your side, too."

Keaven yelled, "You're a Democrat. You're supposed to stand up for protecting women's and immigrants' rights."

Davide replied, "I'm only a Democrat so long as I get re-elected. I need the help of donors like Rosa's foster dad more than I need Rosa's help."

A look of horror appeared on Keaven's face. He replied, "You let her continue to get abused, and I will ensure you're not re-elected by telling the media about what you just did."

Orchard grabbed Keaven in that instant, saying, "I'm not going to lose my meal ticket for white trash like you. I can throw you through that window. You can die, or you can stop talking."

Keaven saw the look of resignation on Rosa's face as she was brought to face her abuser. It was a look he would never forget.

The next day at school, Rosa was not there before the first bell. In fact, she was not there for any of the morning classes. At lunch, the principal announced over the intercom that Rosa had committed suicide and that grief counselors would be available to help students deal with any issues.

Whether she had actually committed suicide or had been killed did not seem to matter much at this point to anybody else. Keaven somehow felt responsible. He was trying to help Rosa. Keaven believed that any decent human being would have helped another in need. His real parents would have.

Of all political parties, the Democrats were supposed to care about the rights of women and minorities. It taught Keaven an important lesson. Words are words. Deeds are deeds. Democrats can say they respect everybody's rights. However, as push came to shove, money mattered more than what was best for American's most oppressed.

School was cancelled the next day so that students could attend Rosa's funeral. Her parents were not allowed to return to the country even for her funeral. Her foster dad did not attend, evidently not caring that such a no-show would make him seem even more guilty. Given the situation then, nobody close to Rosa was present to speak for her. The pastor officiating asked if anybody had anything to say regarding the deceased. Knowing her standing in the school was so low, no student had taken the time to get to know her. There were no options.

Keaven stood up, walked to the front of the church, and finally put himself in front of the microphone. Tears were in his eyes as he began and continued to fall during his entire speech:

"When was it in your life when you first lost your humanity? Was it the first time your parents bought you designer clothes? Was it the first time they said getting to be friends with a son or daughter of an important executive would help them?

Let me help you out with some answers. Every person in this room, whether by rumor, innuendo, or otherwise, knew of the suffering that Rosa endured while she was on earth. Nobody among you did anything.

However, you're not alone in failing her. Government failed her. I failed her. I trusted our elected leaders to care more about those under their watch than getting re-elected.

Rosa had a beautiful soul, more beautiful than the outer appearance of anybody in this room, which is something to which we should all aspire. She endured suffering beyond imagination simply with the false hope that the suffering would lead to being reunited with her family. She hoped it would lead to better lives for others.

What Rosa endured is abominable and is inexcusable. For Rosa's sacrifice, we are given an opportunity we don't deserve in the same way this world was given an opportunity when Christ died on the cross.

I know my path. I know it with more certainty than I have ever known it before. Wherever somebody is suffering, I'll be there. Wherever there's fighting, I'll be there. I cannot be everywhere and help everybody, but I can be somewhere and help somebody.

You can choose your own path, and I won't judge that choice. There is but one final judge. The criteria for judging won't be based on our appearance, clothes, status, cars, or homes. Instead, the criteria will be based on our reaction when encountering somebody who needs our help. Will you look away, or will you stand up together for the least of us?"

As Keaven walked back to his seat, the students refused to make eye contact with him. Many were crying, wiping away tears. Whether it was their collective guilt for not intervening for Rosa or their decision to look away with a decision put to them, Keaven knew his place. He would likely now be the lowest of the low, taking Rosa's place. If doing the right thing meant that you were unworthy, then so be it.

Frankie was waiting to take Keaven, Jessie, and Raul home. Timing can be interesting. Overnight, the Congressman had returned to the Capitol. Government officials called that maneuver the Potomac Two-step. Get out of the fire before you get burned.

Of course, that fact meant that Orchard's rage would be unchecked. Raul interrupted Keaven's thoughts, saying, "I haven't done a good thing for a long time until you allowed me to be part of the plan to help Rosa. I never thought something bad would really happen to her. She needed my help and was right about us being the same. You seemed to be different than Rosa in every way possible but still helped her more than I ever did."

Jessie started crying, saying, "Your words are haunting my soul. I didn't even know I had a soul until today. I feel so guilty. I want to die."

Keaven replied, "You don't want to die. In fact, dying is just the opposite of what Rosa would have wanted. We have to make her death mean something. We cannot let her death pass without taking advantage of the opportunity to change our lives for the better in her memory. Part of that improvement is not allowing anybody else to suffer the fate that she did."

Frankie interjected, "I happened to walk in the church as you were speaking. I feel incredibly guilty for not helping you more, for not standing up for her against your parents even if meant my job. Someday you'll be President."

Keaven commented, "I'll never be President because I care too much about helping people. Presidents have to play the game of pretending to care but end up doing nothing to end suffering anywhere."

Frankie commented, "Don't let Congressman Weiner diminish your faith. He's not every Congressman. He's not even worth half of what you are."

Returning home, Keaven saw his old suitcase, undoubtedly containing his old clothes, positioned on the front step. Orchard said, "Jessie and Raul, in the house. Frankie, you'll be taking Keaven to the airport."

Jessie questioned, "What? He's our brother."

Orchard replied, "He may be your stepbrother, but he's a political liability now. He's going to disappear."

Raul commented, "Wherever he is, I am. We're brothers."

Orchard commanded, "He's going to the United Nations International School in New York City so far away from this political disaster as he can. There's only room for one, so you two are going nowhere."

Orchard said, "Say your final goodbyes."

Jessie commented, "I'm sorry for all the trouble I caused. I'm sorry for burning your Bible and Constitution."

Keaven hugged him, saying, "No worries, brother. What's in my mind and soul cannot be consumed by this earth."

Raul said, "The words you have said today. The change you have brought to me and others will never be forgotten."

Keaven hugged him, saying, "The choice is yours and yours alone how you react to the least of us."

As Keaven climbed into the limousine for what would be the final trip, Jessie said, "If you ever need us, we'll be there."

Raul echoed, "They're not just words. They're a promise."

Jessie mentioned, "By the way, I need to get your Medal of Honor, flag, dog tag, and postcards."

Keaven replied, "Already done." Jessie asked Raul, "How'd he do that? Is he Jesus Christ?"

Keaven answered for him with the window down as the car began to drive out of sight, "Just a son of a former special forces soldier."

As Frankie walked him to his gate for his plane, he handed him a biography about Ronald Reagan. He then said, "Not everybody in California is a liberal. In fact, many aren't liberals. They're just not willing to admit it in public. Read this book. After reading it, you'll no longer believe a President cannot make a difference. If you ever need help that I could provide, let me know. It's been an honor to be in your company."

Keaven hugged Frankie and began walking toward the gate. He was not that used to airplane travel or having to move this quickly from place to place. However, there was always a reason for everything. Maybe there was a reason for learning how to adapt to airplane flights. Only Heaven knew.

9 UNITED NATIONS INTERNATIONAL SCHOOL

The United Nations International School (UNIS) Manhattan campus had provided K-12 education since its formation in 1947. Originally, it was designed to educate kids from families connected with the United Nations, but UNIS had opened up its admission criteria over the years.

Congressman Weiner pulled some strings to get Keaven admitted. It was the least he could do to get a political liability out of the way. With Keaven in New York City, there was not much he could do to ensure a full investigation of Rosa's death in LA.

Further, Davide's attorneys had worked to get Keaven legally emancipated to assure he was no longer an obligation of the Weiner's. His real parent's meager estate was now fully his but would be all that would be available to help fund his life at UNIS.

On final analysis, he could understand why his parents had never spoken of Weiner. Davide was nothing like his real dad, and he could fully comprehend why Darren would not have the time or desire to say a word about him.

At his new school, the principal greeted him first. The conversation turned to staying out of trouble of the type he had caused at Beverly Hills High School. Of course, Keaven defended himself by telling the truth, with which this principal did not seem to want to deal. The principal did mention that the school was having problems with fights. The point was that fighting would not be tolerated, especially from a new student.

Regardless, Keaven was admitted to school in yet another state.

He had so far lived in Texas, Florida, California, and now New York. If he were running for President, that combination would be fruitful in terms of electoral vote counting. However, if he was trying just to fit in, there could be no worse situation.

Keaven's time at UNIS started to pass quickly without many events of significance. Then the fighting really began. The ongoing warfare in the Balkans led to Croats and Serbs fighting in school.

Vlad Purtin, the Russian ambassador's son, seemed to be ever-present, inciting and then watching these conflicts unfold. Keaven tried to intervene the best he could. One day, he put himself between Marina Mikrob, a Serb, and Andrija Horvati, a Croat, who were in the process of beating each other up.

In 1996, Israel attacked Hezbollah in Syria. Arab kids began beating up Jewish kids after school. True to his words in California, Keaven intervened but did so at a high price paid in pounding. He learned for the first time of the benefits of averting unilateral interventions.

With the Middle East at a tipping point, the Middle-Eastern kids were really on edge. The Russian ambassador's son, Vlad Purtin, knew so and wanted to play a trick on them. He lured an Israeli male student, Ehud Shamir, and a Palestinian female student, Shadia Kelani, over to his apartment under the guise of seeking help studying for a test. He refrained from telling them that somebody else would be coming over. He then photographed the two of them together sitting on his bed and sent the pictures over the internet to the Muslim students at UNIS. Vlad intended the pictures to imply something had happened.

All of a sudden, Keaven felt as if history were repeating itself. After hearing of this rumor and about to begin walking home to his apartment, he heard a girl screaming near the school. He knew the shrieks were Shadia's.

He put two and two together and found himself in another situation. Two Muslim students were pinning her against the wall. Another Muslim student was holding a knife, standing directly in front of her. Yet another Muslim student was immediately in front of Keaven, guarding the alley.

Keaven knew what was going on. It was an honor-killing attempt. Families did it to Muslim girls for the girl offending her family's honor. In this circumstance, her alleged dishonor involving an Israeli had somehow been construed as dishonoring all Muslims.

Interestingly enough, the Muslim gang in front of him included many of the individuals who had so recently dispatched of Keaven as he stood against their attack on Jewish students. Ever since Beverly Hills, Keaven had been lifting weights, trying to get stronger. This time, he stood a chance with but four against two.

Although outnumbered, Keaven and Shadia were strong at least in desire. Keaven began talking to the attackers, "Did you notice who sent the pictures? It was Vlad Purtin. Isn't it interesting how he, like Russia, is always stirring up trouble in Middle East?"

The alley guard countered, "Move on. This is our business."

Keaven replied, "I'm sorry, but I can't let a human being get hurt, especially in an exercise intended to protect honor. Just as pride goeth before the fall, so too does honor. You want to kill this girl based on a frame job? You are so willing to believe Vlad yet so unwilling to believe her words. Worse still, your threat to her completely disobeys the Quran and the societal rules in the US."

In a flash as if driven by a force from beyond, Keaven dodged a punch from the alley guard. Keaven tripped him, leaving him on the ground struggling to get back to his feet. Keaven then grabbed the top of a trashcan, using it as a shield to knock away the knife from the attacker in front of Shadia. He next used the shield to knock out the attacker. The two restraining Shadia now grabbed Keaven.

Keaven yelled, "Run for the school, Shadia." She followed orders well, running past the two already on the ground. One of the still-standing attackers left Keaven to chase after her, permitting Keaven to trip the remaining still-standing attacker to the ground.

Keaven was soon dodging past the alley guard, tripping him to the ground for a second time. Keaven reached the attacker pursuing Shadia and tripped him from behind.

Keaven and Shadia ran to the principal's office to explain the situation and ask for help. The police responded, the attackers were expelled, and Keaven had a new admirer.

The level of animosity in the school led Keaven to believe Frankie's words and Reagan's, too. A President could make a difference. He decided to run for President of the student body at UNIS. Vlad Purtin was his opponent. Vlad had believed that he had already bought the vote. There was no way Keaven could win, or so everybody initially thought. Keaven delivered his speech. Four minutes were all that he required, and the oratory changed everything.

He began:

"Today, you face a decision, a choice between good and evil, a choice between peace and war. No, we will not be the ones waging that war at least not now.

Vlad is a person for sure, and any person deserves the opportunity to run for office. However, his platform is one of strife. Mine is of peace, which is peace through strength.

We all know how he tricked Ehud and Shadia into a bad situation just to create more strife. These tricks will continue until we stand together. We have to say we will no longer fight his wars for him. If he wants war, let him fight it by himself.

There is but one simple fact of this world. Evil can only succeed if it divides us. If we are together, evil doesn't stand a chance. Vlad doesn't stand a chance.

No matter what he has promised and provided, nobody has to vote for him. Free men and women have a choice. Today you will make yours in a secret ballot. Your vote will have an effect not just on students here but will be a statement to the UN itself and the world, a statement that can change the world for now and forevermore.

Paraphrasing Dr. Joseph Warren from his 'Boston Massacre Oration,' I say to you: 'Our [world] is in danger but not to be despaired of . . . . Our enemies are numerous and powerful, but . . . Heaven and earth will aid the resolution. On you [rely] the fortunes of [this world]. You are to decide the important questions on which rest the happiness and the liberty of millions yet unborn. Act worthy of yourselves.' We have a choice."

Marina said, "Vlad seeks to divide. Keaven seeks to unite. Easy decision."

Andrija remarked, "While years of war between our nations divide Marina and me, we have no problem agreeing on Keaven as a chance at peace."

Ehud stood up in support, saying, "When I was being beaten up, Keaven intervened and took a pounding for me. Every punch he took was one that I did not have to face. Please support him."

Shadia rose, saying, "My life was in jeopardy, and Keaven, with no concern for his own well-being, put his life on the line to save mine. Please support him." She then kissed him in front of everybody.

While the vote was close, Keaven won in the end. Vlad sulked to the corner, seemingly where evil properly confronted always ends up. All Vlad's maneuvering had failed to divide the students against each other in the end, especially after Keaven's speech of unity.

As Keaven was on his way out, believing himself to be the last person in the room, Vlad remained for a passing comment. He remarked, "Today you've made an enemy for life. So long as I'm alive, you should fear for your life."

Keaven replied, "I don't fear death. Christ died for us all, beating death forevermore."

Vlad responded, "Religion requires useful idiots like you to be successful."

Keaven countered, "It's interesting you say that Vlad because that's exactly what Marx said about Communism. Of course, Russia would never go back to Communism as capitalism fails to gain footing. Would it?"

Vlad commanded, "You should fear me. I'll be President of Russia someday, the most powerful person in the world with the most powerful military in the world."

Keaven replied, "Death brings me closer to the ones I love most, my mother, father, and Rosa. Death threats mean nothing to me."

Vlad continued, "You'll see. Someday you'll be begging me for your life whatever you are saying now. You'll see how powerful I'll become and wish you would have been an ally to me instead of an enemy."

Keaven countered, "When was I ever not your friend? When did I not try to be your friend? You made the choice whether we were friends or enemies. At the end of the day, we're the same except for one key fact. You believe only through the combination of threats and government control of individuals' lives that society can exist effectively. I believe that the combination of freedom and government standing side by side with its citizens enables society to thrive. Until next time, Comrade."

Vlad countered, "You know what all the kids say behind your back. You're white trash."

Keaven replied, "Takes one to know one. Doesn't it?" He then walked away.

While Shadia wanted to date Keaven for no other reason possibly than saving her life, Keaven distanced himself from her because of his experience with Rosa in California. With Vlad after Keaven, any relationship with Shadia could place her at risk for Vlad's retaliation. It was a sad lesson to have to learn, leading to what seemed like perpetual loneliness for Keaven.

Keaven believed it to be for the best anyway. Without much money, Keaven could not be a viable dating option for any girl with any sense. To help pay for rent and school, he had picked up a job as a bike courier after school. With so little time to work while still attending school, Keaven did not earn much.

Because he was deemed an independent contractor instead of an employee, he had to pay 15.3 percent in FICA and Medicare taxes instead of just 7.65 percent. New York state had an income tax as did New York City. He quickly learned lessons on how much any individual ends up working for the government instead of for himself.

While somebody 25-years old with the same job and income would have received an earned income credit around $4,000, Keaven did not get it. The reason was his age and the possibility of still being claimed as a qualifying relative dependent by Davide despite being emancipated. Of course, no elected official cared about this type of discrimination in the Internal Revenue Code. After all, anybody under 18 could not vote and therein was unimportant.

Whereas homeowners could deduct interest and insurance paid on home mortgages, renters were not allowed to deduct the rent they paid. This provision obviously discriminated against the poor and favored the wealthy. Nobody seemed to care that Keaven could have used his rent expense as deductions to help him save some money to better his life. Although Keaven was living below the poverty line, no government entity was there to help him. He had to help himself.

There were still other discriminatory provisions in the Internal Revenue Code, which Keaven soon grew to know based on acquaintances' experiences. Any Mexican national living in the US was eligible for dependency exemptions for each family member that they supported in Mexico. Citizens of Guatemala, El Salvador, Honduras, Nicaragua, Panama, the Caribbean, and South America were ineligible for this provision.

What was the difference between an immigrant from Mexico and from Guatemala? Discrimination based on nationality was supposedly unconstitutional. However, nothing was unconstitutional anymore unless a political lobbying group cared about it. Only the most educated and well advised knew of this exemption, meaning the least knowledgeable, who were the neediest, tended to miss out on this benefit.

Tax policy to the side, Keaven did spend time with Shadia at her house. It was not what the rest of the world thought. He was trying to learn Arabic, nothing more and nothing less then. Something in him said that it would be important to know someday.

Keaven was not necessarily a saint either. As for entertainment, being poor in NYC meant that he had to learn about life in clubs, on urban basketball courts, and in the streets dancing for coins. Again nobody from the government ever seemed to come to Keaven ready and able to provide the proper, if any, assistance. Instead, the government seemed to ignore him while taking money from his pockets that he needed more than the government did to be able to survive.

10 GRADUATION DAY AND BEYOND

Keaven scored 99th percentile on his college admissions exams and graduated first in his class. As such, he won the right to be class valedictorian. In front of an auditorium full of parents, siblings, and relatives with his fellow students and teachers seated behind him, Keaven spoke:

"I know what it is to be rich, not for very long, and to be poor. I know what it is to fit in and not to fit in. I am grateful for the opportunity UNIS has given me. I have met so many individuals who will become this world's next generation of leaders. I have great faith in each one of them.

As we move to the next steps on our paths, I ask us to remember the most important lessons that we've learned. Eyes deceive. They try their best to deceive us into believing we're different. However, ears never deceive. If we truly listen, we can know who a person truly is, the person on the inside, the soul, and you know what? Souls are all the same color and the same nationality. That nationality is world citizen.

While we may choose to see differences in religion, our religions have common precepts. What I'm telling us all today is that, if we remember the days we were able to get along, which far outnumber those days we were not, we will understand that the world of tomorrow is the world of peace. It is not an impossible dream so long as each one of us works together to assure it. There are no limits on what we can each accomplish except for those limits we impose on ourselves.

Friends, teachers, and administrators, I will miss each and every one of you. However, I will forever carry with me the experiences we have shared."

Keaven was on his way to the University of California, Berkeley, a return to the Leftist Coast, set to study political science. He had read enough about Reagan to know Presidents can make a difference. Learning about political science could not do anything but help him achieve his political objectives. Thanks to a full-ride scholarship with his National Merit Scholar status, he would no longer have to worry about working a side job.

He hoped things would be better this time around in Northern California as compared to Southern California. Northern California could not be all about appearance, too. Could it?

The first day of class in Introduction to American Politics, Keaven could tell he was probably on the wrong path. The professor began by saying, "Why do Republicans continue to fight the pro-life battle? They know the majority of the country is pro-choice. It's a losing position."

Keaven raised his hand to answer. Professor Kennedy continued, "The question was meant to be rhetorical." The rest of the class laughed.

Keaven replied, "I'm sorry. I didn't realize that Intro to American Politics would not include any debate in it."

Professor Kennedy, not thrilled, then goaded, "All right then, what's your name?"

Keaven answered, "Keaven."

Professor Kennedy continued, "Keaven, give us your answer."

Keaven responded, "I'm currently an Independent." The class laughed then. Keaven wondered why.

Professor Kennedy helped, "You're on the Leftist Coast. Aren't you? Are there any Republicans in here?"

Nobody raised a hand. Professor Kennedy continued, "How about Independents?"

Keaven was the only student to raise a hand.

Professor Kennedy continued, "Now that you've caveated your statement, please continue."

Keaven mentioned, "Why is the position classified as pro-life? Republicans are in fact just as much pro-choice as Democrats?"

The rest of the class just looked at him like he was from another planet.

Professor Kennedy asked, "What do you mean?"

Keaven continued, "Republicans are pro-choice in that they believe women have a choice whether to engage in certain behavior. Once they make a decision to do so, if you asked the embryo, the fetus, I assure you that the embryo, the fetus, would say it wants to live. In both cases, Republicans respect the rights of those individuals to have their choices respected."

The class laughed. Keaven replied, "What's funny?"

The coed student next to him raised her hand, "Is there any way I can change my seat? I didn't think I'd have to sit next to a redneck at Berkeley."

Keaven questioned, "Isn't it interesting that somebody has no problem referencing the color of somebody's skin if the words are 'redneck'? However, the same person probably has great problems with an NFL franchise in Washington, DC, continuing to use virtually the same descriptor. That is called hypocrisy."

The coed student looked at him and said, "You must be from the South."

Keaven replied, "You must be from Hypocrisyville. Nice to meet you."

Professor Kennedy replied, "Calm down, everybody. Please calm down."

Keaven felt as if he were on an island in the middle of the Pacific Ocean. He was not committed to being a Republican yet, but where was the respect in this world for an Independent or even healthy political debate with a would-be Republican?

Professor Kennedy replied, "Science has educated us that an embryo or a fetus has no ability to make choices, so your overstatement of the ability of an embryo or a fetus to make choices is an inappropriate argument."

Keaven asked, "How about the characterization of women having a choice whether to engage in the initial behavior?"

"The Constitution guarantees the protection of women's right to privacy to make such decisions regarding their body," Professor Kennedy continued.

Having memorized the Constitution himself, Keaven replied, "What article uses those words?"

Professor Kennedy answered, "Don't tell me you believe in strict constructionism." The class again laughed.

Keaven replied, "I believe that the words in the Constitution are the highest level of authority to decide legal questions in this country, and the Supreme Court seems to agree with me whether they are conservative or liberal."

Professor Kennedy commented, "Of course, the Supreme Court agrees with me in the right to abortions."

Keaven countered, "Much of the world believed the sun revolved around the earth even with evidence to the contrary. How much easier is it then for a Supreme Court to read into a vague document a right that doesn't seem guaranteed anywhere directly in the Constitution?"

Professor Kennedy replied, "Interestingly enough, the clock says that it's time for class to end. Until next time, students."

After class, Professor Kennedy waited to Keaven to be alone in the room with him, saying, "I'd encourage you to change majors. I respect a worthy debater, but I don't want conflicts in my class. My student evaluations will not be great if they continue. You're the instigator, so again I'd ask kindly, for your benefit and mine, that you drop this class and the major."

Keaven questioned, "If I don't then?"

"You'll fail," Professor Kennedy remarked.

Keaven was not a quitter. He loved a challenge, especially if right were on his side. However, it was obvious that learning a subject matter in a place so hostile to his point of view would not be conducive to learning. Keaven's new major soon became Economics.

If it was good enough for Reagan, then the major was good enough for him.

At the same time he was in the registrar's office, he saw a familiar face from class, a guy who was sitting on his other side during the entire debate.

He introduced himself as "God."

Keaven replied, "Are you kidding me?"

"God" replied, "It's my online name for gaming and communication purposes. It sounds so much better than Maurice."

Keaven countered, "How about I call you, Mo?"

Mo commented, "It works."

Keaven replied, "What are you doing here now?"

Mo intoned, "I've lived in San Francisco, not any suburb, but San Francisco for my whole life. There is no such thing as a Constitution. The word illegal does not exist in describing anything that advances the liberal, Democratic agenda, at least in this area. I'd hoped college would be different. I'm a Republican in a land of Democrats."

Keaven countered, "There are worse afflictions. You could be a Communist living in the South or a religious zealot like the Dalai Lama living under Chinese oppression."

Mo replied, "Isn't that Dalai Lama situation interesting? All the Hollywood elite liberals, who don't believe in God, somehow believe with all their might in the Dalai Lama, a religious figure, and religious freedom. At the same time, they belittle anybody of faith in this country."

Keaven continued, "Hypocrisy is certainly interesting, especially coming from a Democratic party that says it is the only party based on logic."

"My Dad's a top executive at Apple," Mo continued. "Because of the connections I have in the technology world, I'm the best hacker in the world."

"Hacking's a crime, Mo," Keaven countered.

"Only if you get caught," Mo answered. He continued, "Besides, again nobody here seems to follow any rules that diminish their causes, so why should I? That's why I'm a Republican. Counterculture here is being a Republican. It's the new cool. It's the new rule."

Keaven answered, "Rules are rules for a reason."

Mo answered, "Ends justify the means. If Democrats can use the argument, then I can, too."

"I guess we agree to disagree on that point," Keaven continued. "Still good, though, to meet another good soul."

Mo continued, "I'm changing my major to computer science. I tried political science because I already know more than the computer science professors and wanted to learn more about politics. However, I suppose there's always something I don't know about computer programming. I can't imagine what that might be, but it is at least possible."

Keaven ended, "We'll stay in touch."

Mo replied, "If you ever need something hacked, let me know. Nothing can stop God, and God is a Republican."

11 THE POWER

In his new Introduction to Economics class, Keaven first noticed the gal sitting next to him. She was conversing with the gal next to her, her roommate. It was the twang in her voice. It reminded him of his time living in the South, Texas and Florida certainly. There was not much Southern accent in Florida, but you could find it to the extent you wanted to do so. Suddenly, Keaven attempted to recoup that accent, asking her, "How long have you been liberated from the South?"

The gal sternly replied, "Are you making fun of my Southern accent?"

Surprised at the reaction, Keaven countered in straight, Midwestern English, "No, I just wanted to show off that I could be equally cool as you are."

She asked, "Are you from the South, too?"

Keaven replied, "By way of Ft. Hood and AFB MacDill. That's Texas and Florida."

A smile coming to her face, she answered, "I'm Tricia by way of Ft. Bragg and AFB MacDill."

Pleasantly surprised at learning of a fellow MacDiller, Keaven replied, "What years did you live at MacDill?"

Tricia responded, "1994 to 1996. My dad was a replacement for some special forces soldiers who died in Somalia."

Keaven could not hide the look of sadness on his face. Tricia questioned, "What's wrong?"

"My father died in the Battle of Mogadishu in 1993," he stated, tears forming in his eyes.

"I'm sorry," Tricia countered.

Keaven continued, "You didn't say anything wrong. I'm sorry for the tears here. Guys from the South are not supposed to cry. I know."

"So do you like listening to Shania Twain?" Tricia continued.

"I know I enjoy looking at Shania Twain," Keaven countered.

She put her hand on his shoulder and responded, "At least I know you're interested in girls, so now I can tell you that you're cute."

He replied, "I'm no Ronald Reagan."

Tricia countered, "You better be quiet. You could get us in trouble mentioning him."

In fact, Keaven's mentioning of Ronald Reagan suddenly did stop the conversation in the room. A student in the back questioned, "Did I just hear somebody mention a former good-for-nothing President?"

Some fights were worth fighting. Still others were not. This fight was not worth it.

Keaven told Tricia, "I know what you mean. What a surprising reaction given he was the governor of California, their own nation as it seems here in SF. Changing the conversation to something more positive, I'd like to ask you how you came to be at Berkeley?"

Tricia responded, "I'm here on a gymnastics scholarship."

Keaven looked at her again with surprise, "You must be at least 5' 9"."

Tricia continued, "I know that I'm tall for a gymnast. It makes it more difficult."

"You'll have no problem getting a date even being from the South," Keaven continued.

"What do you mean?" Tricia mentioned.

"If it isn't too sexist to say it this way, gymnasts are hot, and, among gymnasts, well, you're a supernova," Keaven replied.

"You must not have asked many girls out in your lifetime," Tricia replied with a smile.

Professor Edmundson began class, "Today, we're going to discuss government macroeconomic policy with an emphasis on the failings of Reaganomics."

Tricia and Keaven just looked at each other, wry smiles on their faces. Yes, it was the Leftist Coast after all. Even though Reagan was a Californian in many ways, Republicans were evidently strangers in a strange land.

After class, Keaven resolved not to change majors, especially because of the presence of Tricia. This decision became irreversible once Tricia slipped him a note with her number, saying, "I'm a Republican, too, and I play soccer, too, dual-sport athlete that I am. Why don't you come watch us this Friday against Cal Poly? If we win, we'll have a team party after. You're invited."

While he was officially an Independent, he was not going to argue with a supernova gymnast and soccer player. Life could be worse.

Email and the internet were relatively new things to Keaven. However, he checked his email and found a message from Mo:

"Do you want to form a College Republicans Club? We could stir up some trouble with the College Democrats Club."

Keaven replied, "Why don't you come watch the Cal women's soccer team this Friday at 4:00?"

Mo replied immediately:

"Thanks, but I'd rather hack the DNC's website. Well, I guess I did that yesterday. I suppose, but I'm not too much into sports."

Keaven countered, "We can use it as an opportunity to discuss strategic options against the evil empire. Until then."

Keaven was not much of a phone person, so he emailed Tricia:

"I didn't know quite what to expect coming to Berkeley, but you alone have made me feel like this place is right for me."

Tricia replied, "Right is might. I can't wait for Friday night."

The Cal Bears beat Cal Poly, so the party was on. It was a house party with a DJ. EDM was a relatively new genre for Keaven, but he had started to get used to it in NYC.

The only word that came to mind in describing Tricia was "unbelievable." She had scored the winning goal in a one to nothing triumph. She was a striker but was a true freshman just like Keaven. She could really dance, which was to be expected with floor exercise in gymnastics basically constituting tumbling and dancing. Keaven was certainly no Fred Astaire.

Mo tagged along, lugging his laptop and hacking who knows what. There were more guys than gals in the room unfortunately, and, of course, all the guys wanted to get with Tricia, the star, the object of all the attention.

At one point, some of Tricia's teammates came up to her, whispered in her ear, and motivated her to say out loud and discernible to everybody in the room, "My teammates say the guy I'm dancing with is not good enough for me, so I'll give him one last chance to prove himself."

Mo suddenly looked up from his laptop. Every eye in the room was now on Keaven. While he was surprised and caught off guard, Keaven never shirked from a call of duty. By the way then, he did have a secret weapon from growing up in the streets of New York City, breakdancing.

"DJ, cue up 'Unbelievable' in honor of Tricia who is a supernova and in honor of an NYC tradition, breakdancing," Keaven confidently remarked. He cleared an area of the floor of people, grabbed a stocking cap from his pocket, put it on his head, and, with the beginning refrains of "Unbelievable," began breakdancing.

Long before the song's end, the entire room was cheering him on. After the song finished, Mo reached him first and grabbed him by the arm. He said, "That was the coolest display of dancing I've ever seen. Teach me, great master."

"Later, Mo," Keaven remarked.

Tricia kissed him, moving to a hug and asking everybody in the room, "So what's the verdict? Is he good enough for me?"

One of her teammates replied, "He's too good for you, but he's good enough for me." Everybody started laughing.

Tricia walked Keaven out to the front porch, quite possibly to prevent her teammates from stealing him away. The result was some alone time together.

Sitting on a grungy couch with Tricia and looking up at the sky,

Keaven began, "You have to watch the public displays of affection. You could start to get me a bad reputation."

"Who says that Republicans can't be cool and hot?" Tricia responded. "How'd you learn to dance like that? It's cool. It's hot."

"The streets of New York City," Keaven replied with a little sigh, remembering the good times but also the bad times.

"How many places have you lived?" Tricia questioned, surprised at his connection to NYC.

Keaven responded, "Texas, Florida, California, New York, back to California, so I guess really four different places."

Tricia asked, "Are you trying to get electoral votes or something?"

Keaven replied with exasperation, "It seems that, every time I bring up where I've lived, politics always enter the conversation."

"To him to whom much has been given, much is expected," Tricia replied.

They were both then looking at the full moon in the sky. Keaven said, "Can you believe there was a time we thought we'd never get to the moon? Then JFK made it a priority, and eventually it happened. I don't know. I constantly go through whether one person can make any difference. With the Republican Revolution in Congress, so many changes were promised. However, how many have been delivered because of a Democrat in the White House? George Washington wanted us to work together for what is right. He abhorred the notion of parties. I sometimes believe he's right. There's no left or right."

Tricia finished the statement, "There is only right."

Keaven intoned, "Why did God make you so perfect?'

Tricia replied, "You'd better be careful about bringing up God here, too. I'm not sure who is hated more on this coast, God, Ronald Reagan, or an average Republican."

Keaven continued, "Come on. You can answer the question."

Tricia countered, "It's just a pick-up line like Heaven's missing an angel, you."

"Nobody's perfect," Tricia continued. "I scored but one goal, not 100. I don't get perfect scores in every gymnastics rotation."

Keaven continued, "I don't know. There's just a great weight that I carry. I guess that I feel like I have all these expectations placed on me. I sometimes wonder whether I'll be able to live up to them all."

"You don't even know how to date," Tricia mentioned, continuing, "You're supposed to get the girl excited for a second date. You're acting as if we've been dating for a year."

Keaven replied, "I'm sorry. I wear my emotions on my sleeves. I don't pull any punches."

Tricia took over the conversation, mentioning, "When I look at the moon, I see peace. I see hope for the future. I see beauty."

"What's your dream?" Keaven countered.

"I don't know you that well yet," Tricia replied.

"Look. I didn't ask you what your fantasy was. I just asked about your dream," Keaven continued.

"What's your dream?" Tricia coyly asked.

"I asked first," Keaven replied.

"I asked better," Tricia responded.

All of a sudden, Keaven flashed back to a similar conversation with Rosa. He soon showed a look of resignation on his face.

Tricia had to shake him to get him out of his trance. Tricia asked, "What's wrong?"

Keaven replied, "I've had this conversation before, and let's just say that things did not work out from that point onward."

Tricia saw how glum and grave Keaven had become. To cheer him up, she revealed, "I've never felt a connection with somebody like I have with you. It's as if we were destined to meet. It's as if we'd known each other for years. I can talk to you like I can't talk with anybody else."

Keaven's visage did not change. Tricia hoped that it would. She continued, "Is it because I won't share my dream with you?"

"No, it's not that," Keaven replied with a thousand-yard gaze, still remembering Rosa and his failure to save her.

"Let's make a deal," Tricia began. "You share with me what's troubling you so that I can help you overcome it, and I'll share with you what my dream is."

For a moment, a spark returned to Keaven, and he replied, "You do know what my last name is. Right? 'Let's make a deal': Think about what you just said."

Keaven started laughing. Tricia laughed, too. She mentioned with resignation, "Sorry. I kind of walked into that one."

Keaven continued, "All right. This Deal is making a deal with you, but just remember: You asked for it."

Tricia replied with a smile, "All right just so long as you don't tell me you're an ax murderer."

"A couple of years ago in SoCal, I was attending Beverly Hills High School and met a girl, Rosa," Keaven began. "Everybody else had stigmatized her not necessarily because she was an undocumented alien or because she had a foster dad but instead because her foster dad was abusing her."

Keaven stopped for a moment, tears coming to his eyes. He continued: "I didn't know any of the tales, but I could just tell she was getting abused. I brought her home the first chance I could, thinking my stepparents would help me get her to safety. Instead, they brought her foster dad over to take her back. The next day, she either committed suicide or was murdered. Nobody wanted to investigate because her foster dad was a prominent celebrity. Sadly, the foster dad did not change his ways and is in prison right now on a sexual assault conviction. Another woman was brave enough to speak up and fight back against a celebrity. It is the greatest failure of my life that I was not able to save Rosa. From that point onward, wherever I've seen suffering, I've intervened. It's like having to pay a penance that I'll never be able to satisfy. I'll never be able to do enough good to bring her back. I'll never be able to do enough good to save my soul."

Tricia put her arm around him, trying to comfort him in response to all the tears. She intoned, "The way it sounds to me, you tried to help somebody with all the power you had. Others had a chance to help but did not intervene. They're the ones who should have a guilty conscience, not you."

Keaven replied, "You don't have to answer the dream question.

This has been the worst first date you've ever had in your life. I apologize for ruining what should have been a festive atmosphere. You deserve far better than me." Keaven stood up to walk away, breaking her embrace.

"Don't leave," Tricia implored. "You don't have to carry this burden or any other burdens you have alone."

"Thanks, but your teammates were right. You do deserve somebody better," Keaven remarked, and he was off walking into the night. Keaven had learned a lesson from Rosa and in fact from his parents: Do not get attached to anybody, let alone fall in love with anybody. That way, you don't have to deal with the hurt if God takes them away from you.

Keaven somehow remembered from UNIS history class that Truman used to take long walks. He wondered how much longer those walks were after Truman decided to drop the atomic bombs on Hiroshima and Nagasaki.

At the same time he had that thought, Keaven also considered the dilemma that was his life: Why did everything always have to be related to politics? Why could he not just enjoy college life like every other college student?

It then hit him perhaps for the first time. Some were destined to stand guard like an owl that he had just seen perched in a tree. Some were meant never to enjoy their lives but instead to watch out for others so that they may enjoy theirs. It was a pretty grim assessment of his future. However, it seemed true.

Somebody had to stand guard to allow the others to enjoy their lives. His father had stood guard, never asking for personal joy but instead sacrificing for his country. He looked up at the great horned owl, saying, "Good to know that I'm not the only one on guard."

Once home, Keaven looked at his emails, four from Mo and none from Tricia. Keaven considered the evidence. It obviously meant that Tricia was wise beyond her years and had returned to the party. She would easily pick up another very likely better replacement for company than Keaven. All was well that ended well.

Things were fitting into place at least in some ways. Well, they were not really. Tricia was a supernova, probably a stupid adjective but the best he could do at the moment and carry forward. Keaven really liked her, but he of course had really liked Rosa and Shadia, too. Oh, well, Keaven considered.

He read Mo's first email: "I overheard your entire conversation with Tricia. You're an idiot by the way. Do you know how lucky you are to find a Republican girl in California, let alone somebody so unbelievable? I've been dancing with her this whole time to save her for you. I can't dance by the way. I can't type very fast. Have to get back to dancing with her. Guys are moving in. Get your tail over here before I get pummeled."

Mo's second email went: "It really takes that long to walk back to your residence? Get over here."

Mo's next email was: "I can't dance anymore. I'm exhausted. I took Tricia back out to the porch to share information I've hacked on your background to make her interested and get me some rest. Get over here."

Mo's final email was: "Have you ever stopped to consider how wonderful I am as a friend? You owe me big time, and, by the way, GET OVER HERE NOW!!!!!!!!!!!!"

Just as Keaven was about to run out the door, there was a knock on it. He opened the door and saw Mo and Tricia standing in front of him.

Mo rushed past to lie down on Keaven's couch, laptop on top of him. Tricia gave Keaven a great big hug, saying, "I didn't realize you'd been through so much in your life."

Mo came to life, "How is it that you were able to get an off-campus apartment as a first-year? They wouldn't let me have that option."

Keaven replied, "I'm just used to living on my own and found a way like I always seem to do."

"By the way, Mo, how did you find out where I lived? The student directory is not out yet," Keaven angrily demanded.

"The code of a hacker is never to share one's secrets," Mo replied.

"What do you know about me from hacking, and what did you tell Tricia?" Keaven commanded.

Mo replied, "Well, if I tell you what I know from hacking you with Tricia still standing here, then she'll know everything then, too. Thus, your second question would be rendered irrelevant."

Tricia replied, "I know about what Jessie and Raul did to you. I know about what Davide and Orchard did to you. I know what you said at Rosa's funeral. I know what you did and said at UNIS."

Keaven asked, "But how?"

Mo replied, "With the internet have come blogs. Everybody has a blog. The words you have said have such an impact on individuals that they remember the conversations for the rest of their lives. Jessie and Raul wrote about profound regret for treating you the way they did. There are some kids of some pretty famous Hollywood types, who mention your words in their blogs, on their sites. In fact, some of those kids are pretty famous in of themselves."

Tricia interpreted, "What he is getting at is you have a power inside you, a charisma, an energy, an insight to change individuals for the better."

Keaven replied, "I don't have any power."

Mo intoned, "You're like Jesus Christ with the power of mind control. Your words are hypnotizing."

Keaven responded, "Well, okay. If that is meant as a positive, then thanks.'

Tricia answered the question, "My dream is to be First Lady."

Keaven let that thought sink in and then responded, "There was a time in my life where I would have been insulted by that comment in the sense that you wanted to use me to get to the White House. I am at a point in my life where I do not consider that dream to be akin to gold digging. I can live with that so long as you are genuinely interested in me and acknowledge the odds of me becoming President are less than me winning the lottery."

Mo interrupted, "Wow. For being a Republican, you sound about as boring as Al Gore. Regardless, you've already won the lottery by finding Tricia, so I guess that means 'Hail to the Chief' should be the next words out of my mouth."

Keaven replied, "You're kind, Mo, but you can be slightly irritating sometimes."

Mo replied, "I want to be your campaign manager."

Tricia responded, "I want to be your wife."

Keaven answered, "Both of you are caught up in the moment and are saying things you don't really mean."

Time passed quickly, and soon it was the winter holiday break. Mo and Tricia were ready to travel home for the holidays. Of course, Keaven had no reason to travel. Nobody was left in his family, so he would be alone for the break.

"Before we leave for the break, we wanted to ease your loneliness," Tricia ventured.

"What do you mean?" Keaven replied.

"I bought this singing Christmas tree for you," Tricia replied. "You'll at least have a Christmas tree. It might be the only one in all San Francisco for how it's not politically correct to have a Christmas tree anymore."

Mo said, "Here you go, Keaven." Mo handed him a CD. "It's every important Ronald Reagan speech he ever made."

Tricia replied, "I'd love to take you with me, but . . . ."

Keaven interrupted, "Plane tickets cost a lot of money. I haven't asked to marry you or anything, so it would be stupid to introduce me to your parents."

Mo intoned, "I'd ask you if you'd want to come with me, but I assure you that I live in the most liberal home in the world. It's hell for me and would be hell for you. My father won't even let me watch O'Reilly and Hannity."

"I feel like an idiot because I really didn't get either of a present," Keaven replied.

Tricia countered, "Don't worry about it. We know how tight money is for you without any family to help support you."

"It's pretty cheap of me, but I did make Christmas cards for each of you," Keaven said, handing them to Mo and Tricia.

Tricia's had Keaven's best rendition of Santa Claus on the front of the card. Inside, he drew Santa Claus's bag. The note written inside said, "To the most beautiful woman in the world on the inside and outside: I hope someday to help all your dreams come true. Until then, keep your faith in me. You have made me feel not only welcome here but also stronger than any foe."

To Mo, Keaven had crafted a Christmas tree on the front cover of the card. Inside, Keaven had drawn a present. The inscription then included the following: "With God's help, someday this Christmas present will be unwrapped to show a Republican President in office."

Tricia hugged Keaven and then kissed him. Keaven remarked, "Hey, there's no mistletoe here for a reason."

Mo hugged Keaven, saying, "You're the best friend I could ever hope to have. Together we'll make this present come true someday."

"Before you leave, do you have enough time to watch O'Reilly and Hannity with me? They're talking about some important stuff tonight," Keaven implored.

Tricia replied, "My flight leaves later tonight. I'll get home early morning, not ideal, but it saved me some serious travel expenses leaving that late."

Mo answered, "With my father denying me the opportunity to watch at home, why would I turn down the opportunity here?"

"Besides, O'Reilly and Hannity are really cute," Tricia answered. "I wouldn't miss them for the world."

Mo interjected, "I wish I were O'Reilly or Hannity."

"Don't worry, Mo. I'll find a girl for you," Tricia replied.

Keaven felt like this gathering was the happiest of his life since his parents had passed away. He took out a camera and took a picture of Tricia and Mo on the couch watching Fox.

Mo then said, "We need a picture of you two love birds."

He rose to his feet, told them to slide closer together on the couch, and then said, "Tricia, pretend that there's mistletoe above you."

Before Keaven could open his mouth to say, "Come on, Mo. Not again," Tricia was kissing him. Mo took the picture, laughing for a few seconds.

As O'Reilly and then Hannity respectively went off the air, Mo left first. Keaven said, "You are the best friend a guy could ever have."

Mo replied, "What would you expect from God?"

Soon he was off to his home. Tricia and Keaven were left together just for a few moments before she would have to leave to pack and take a cab to the airport.

"Don't worry. I'll be back soon. I can't be gone long because of gymnastics," Tricia intoned.

"I wish I could bottle this night up and live it over and over again for the rest of my life," Keaven replied.

"What makes you think this night will be the best you ever live? There are so many more nights left in our lives, so much promise, so much potential," Tricia responded.

With that expression, Tricia was out the door. Indeed, she had to pack more clothes and call the cab to the airport.

Keaven wondered why he just had a feeling that this night would be the most joyful of his life. Was he too fatalistic? Was he too used to tragedy? Oh, well, he was left to watch television alone.

12 CHEL COLTON

Time passed quickly, and soon the Keaven, Mo, and Tricia grouping had a new challenge on the Leftist Coast. President Colton's daughter decided to enroll at a nearby university. To make matters worse, she instantly wanted to make an impression that she was her own woman. Chel was leading a student protest march against Operation Desert Fox, a Colton ordered bombing of Iraq, in December 1998. The bombing campaign lasted four days in response to ongoing Iraqi violations of UN Security Council Resolutions. Chel was on hand from the second day onward.

Keaven, Tricia, and Mo, still best of friends, resolved to protest against their protest. Keaven carried a US flag. Tricia had a placard, saying "Support Operations that Make Our Troops Safer." While constantly wrapped up in his laptop, Mo enjoyed the opportunity to shout: "God is a Republican, and Right Makes Might."

Chel certainly noticed them that third day of the bombing campaign. She came over, with her mob of supporters in tow, saying, "War is hell, so anybody who believes in might does not believe in God."

Tricia questioned, "Do you believe in God, Chel?"

Ignoring the question, Chel said, "I'll ask you to leave before I call the police to have you removed."

Mo responded, "Are you kidding me? The San Francisco police haven't arrested a protester for 30 years."

Chel replied, "That's because nobody was ever stupid enough to protest as a Republican. You're instigating a riot, not protesting."

Keaven replied, "What riot?"

A gigantic Cal offensive lineman came forward, saying, "The riot that happens as we stomp on you."

Tricia replied, "Big surprise. A protest supposedly in support of peace resorts to violence."

Chel surely enough dialed 911 on her designer phone. At least she did it herself instead of relying on her Secret Service detail to do so.

As the police came, Keaven, Tricia, and Mo felt no fear. They were equally allowed to protest as these liberals were. Might unfortunately made right. Chel's family name and cries of instigating a riot somehow led to the police taking away Keaven, Tricia, and Mo.

Keaven questioned, "You can't be serious. How in any way are we instigating a riot?"

The police officer leading Keaven away mentioned, "We're actually saving you from a beating."

Tricia replied, "We're not afraid of peace protesters."

Mo questioned, "Are we under arrest?" He was worried about his Apple executive parent somehow taking away his computing privileges. He could always hack back in but certainly did not want to have to deal with his liberal father any more than he had to do so.

Keaven's minder replied, "No, you're not under arrest so long as you agree not to face off against these peace protesters again."

Keaven asked, "What about freedom of speech?"

His minder commented, "Haven't you learned that, in California, there's only freedom of speech if you're a liberal?"

Mo replied, "I suppose that's why you send city workers out the next day to cover up pro-Republican graffiti but leave up the pro-Democrat graffiti."

Keaven's minder answered, "When in Rome, what do you think you are supposed to do?"

As they were finally set free from handcuffs four blocks away from the protest scene, Keaven replied, "Maybe everybody in this world cowers in the face of a Colton, but I never will. Chel may have won the battle, but she'll never win the war."

Keaven continued, "At least not so long as God is on our side."

Mo corrected, "At least not so long as we get the press on our side. We should have called them to photograph our demonstration of the demonstration."

"Chel thinks she's so cool," Tricia intoned. "She's nothing but a wanna-be. If it weren't for her father being in the White House, she wouldn't have been admitted to school out here."

Keaven remarked, "Don't demean her too much. She has some base-level intelligence."

Tricia, with a mix of jealousy and rage in her eyes, countered, "So have you fallen in love with her already like every other guy out here?"

Keaven replied, "I predict I'll be able to change her someday. Her mother was a Republican and became a Democrat. I can make her a Republican."

Mo, tapping Keaven on the shoulder, mentioned, "Remember. You're still a registered Independent. What don't you start with trying to make her an Independent?"

Tricia countered, "Why don't you both stop bothering with her?"

Mo demanded, "Why are you so scared of her getting our attention?"

Tricia replied, "She's beautiful, powerful, connected, and rich."

"The measure of a person is what is on the inside, the content of the character," Keaven replied. "As I encountered her, I saw her soul. It's empty. It's our challenge to fill it with purpose, our purpose."

Tricia countered, "You might as well be Don Quixote."

Mo interjected, "That's the way of thinking, implying she's the prostitute from Don Quixote."

Tricia continued, "No, I meant it as Keaven here, Don Quixote, is twisting at windmills again."

"The bottom line is that she doesn't have your beautiful soul," Keaven opined to Tricia.

"Save the pick-up lines," Tricia replied. "I'm going to leave to work on my floor exercise routine."

Mo happily said, "I love watching you on the floor exercise."

Keaven grabbed Mo, saying, "I have other plans for you tonight."

"Suit yourselves," Tricia replied. "Bye, Mo," Tricia said, blowing Mo a kiss. She continued, "Maybe I'm dating the wrong guy."

Mo smiled. Keaven did not.

With Tricia gone, Keaven walked with Mo back to Keaven's apartment. Once there, Keaven began, "Think how many converts we could get if we could get Chel on our side."

"Didn't you once say that the devil's not to be played with or trifled with?" Mo replied.

"You saw how charismatic she was out there today, leading her protest," Keaven countered.

Mo questioned, "Are you sure you're not falling for her? Hey, it's ok if you are. I wouldn't mind dating Tricia."

"She was protesting her own father's decision," Keaven mentioned. "That fact has to count for something, saying that she is receptive to different ideas."

Mo commented, "You're just setting yourself up for heartbreak. When push comes to shove, we all revert back to the culture in which we were raised. She's a Democrat, and you could lose Tricia in the process. That's a lose-lose."

Keaven countered, "You don't and won't revert back to your father's extreme liberalism."

"I'm special," Mo replied.

Keaven continued, "That you are, Mo. That's why you have to figure out her email address. It's not in the student directory evidently to protect her privacy."

Mo reluctantly replied, "I suppose you'll want her phone number and address, too."

Keaven answered, "Now that you mention it."

"Take a look," Mo quickly stated. "Done and done. In fact, I didn't even have to hack anything."

Hugging him, Keaven replied, "I'm proud of you, Mo."

"Hacking's an addiction that I'm trying my best to break, thanks to you," Mo responded.

Mo continued, "Whatever your motives are, be careful. Tricia's really special. Don't lose her. You'll never forgive yourself. Be careful because Chel is not stupid. There's a reason why her parents attended Yale for graduate work. Even though they may be devils in human disguises, they certainly are not lacking for intelligence or for an ability to trick any political opponent. You'd be a fool to believe those traits weren't passed on to Chel."

"I always appreciate the vote of confidence, Mo," Keaven sarcastically replied.

"You can go watch Tricia at the gym now," Keaven continued.

"Thanks, Dad," Mo said sarcastically, busy with his laptop as he walked away on his way to the gym.

Keaven began writing an email to Chel: "I was the leader of the opposition group today. I'd love to meet you in person sometime to make up for causing you any difficulty. Who knows? Maybe we could bat around some political ideas. Keaven Deal"

A response came back quickly, "You're the first person out here to ask me out on a date. I admire the courage. I accept. Tomorrow 5:00 PM."

Keaven promptly typed and sent, "But where?"

Just as quickly, Chel replied, "If you already know my email, you already know my address. Am I right?"

Keaven did not respond to the rhetorical question. He suddenly pondered whether he had overestimated his gift to change people and underestimated hers. It was not necessarily that often that Keaven doubted himself.

Tricia then emailed, saying, "I thought you'd come looking for me at some point. Is anything wrong? Can we have dinner tomorrow at 5:00 PM?"

Keaven replied, "Busy. Why don't you have dinner with Mo?"

Maybe Mo was right. Maybe he was risking a bird in the hand for two in the bush.

Keaven opened the jewelry box with the ring he had bought for Tricia. He had saved up for a long time to be able to buy it, and it was "the ring."

Mo knew about it. In fact, God knew about everything. What could Keaven expect from him reading every message he sent or received on his laptop?

Oh, well, there was no room for retreat now. He was working for the greater good anyway.

13 WHO'S CONTROLLING WHOM HERE?

The first thing that surprised Keaven was how modest Chel's room was. She was not the spoiled brat that the press had made her out to be. The second thing that amazed Keaven was how young Chel's two Secret Service personnel were. They looked and dressed like typical college students. The two patted Keaven down for weapons and then agreed to leave Keaven and Chel alone in their room.

"Why were you interested in asking me on a date?" Chel began, certainly curious for the answer.

"I'm sure you're expecting me to say because I worship your father," Keaven started. "However, nothing could be farther from the truth despite our protest the other day in support of a policy he had commanded."

"Explain," Chel commanded.

"With all due respect, are you trying to psychoanalyze me or something akin to it?" Keaven replied.

Chel gleefully acknowledged, "Any girl has to be impressed with a guy who mentions the word 'respect,' has the intelligence to use 'psychoanalyze' properly, and reads enough historical fiction to use 'akin' in these times. In addition, I admire the fact you're willing to speak your Republican mind in a sea of liberals."

Keaven wondered why he had the compulsion to do so. He never did with Tricia. He still had not properly explained to Tricia how committed he was to being an Independent. However, something about Chel put him at ease, maybe too much at ease. He now wanted to explain that he was actually an Independent and why he was.

"I'm an Independent and proud to be because it's what George Washington and Ronald Reagan believed in," Keaven mentioned.

Chel responded, "I'm a Democrat who is willing to bend to the far left if necessary to fit in here."

She continued, "Believe it or not, a moderate Democrat like me didn't believe I could ever find a moderate anywhere. So far, everybody who has sought my heart or whatever it is that they are seeking has come at me as a left-winger. How is it that nobody sees my father for who he is, a moderate Democrat? How is it that they then don't see me as a moderate Democrat?"

Keaven, resigned to defeat with knowledge of her true affiliation, which he should have assumed from the start, replied, "I'm sorry for bothering. I'll leave you to your moderate Democrat world."

Chel laughed, saying, "Didn't you hear what I was saying? It's not a huge leap from being an Independent to being a moderate Democrat. They're virtually identical. Besides, I like you."

"Unfortunately, the gulf between Independent and moderate Democrat is far wider for me than you may expect," Keaven acknowledged.

"Let me reiterate for the intellectually impaired," Chel ironically countered. "I like you. Why do politics have to matter?"

Keaven stopped to consider the situation for a second. He had a power in him in which he and others believed. It was the power to change individuals into seeing politics differently. Could he still change Chel and make her a useful ally, a powerful ally, in his cause? Was he now playing a game that he should not be playing?

Chel playfully countered, "There's nothing to think about. You have a wonderful girl interested in you."

Keaven sacrificed his beliefs, saying, "You're right. Politics are nothing. If Independents and moderate Democrats can't get along, then how can we ever believe in peace through strength?"

Chel replied, "You mean peace through peace. You'll see. I'll get you politically correct once I've had some time to work on you. Shoot me an email tomorrow night at 9:00 PM. I'll ditch the security detail, and we'll head into the city. You can be a personal guide for a new girl not used to the clubs in this city."

Keaven countered, "Most clubs are 21 only."

Chel answered, "That's no problem for a President's daughter."

Keaven replied, "There's a reason they're 21 only."

Chel commented, "Don't worry. Colton's can handle their liquor."

Keaven continued with reservations, "I didn't necessarily think you were a party girl."

"What do you expect from me after I've been imprisoned in the White House all my teenage life?" Chel ruefully replied.

"I'm not necessarily a party guy," Keaven lamented.

"Don't worry. I can change you for the better. Call me tomorrow. Jace and Susana, are you listening?" Chel commented.

With no response coming from them, Chel commented, "Good. They didn't hear the plan. See you tomorrow." As she literally was throwing him out the door, she kissed him and, worse still, took a digital picture of it to post on the internet.

Chel continued, "Again don't worry. I prefer to have the press write about my new love interest as opposed to the protesting. My Dad gave me a lecture about the protest and being unified as a family once he saw it on the news. He said that I should find somebody to date and get my mind off politics. I agreed. He was right as always."

Keaven could only think, "No, he was left as he always was." He then turned to consider how he was going to explain to Tricia and later Mo the picture that would undoubtedly soon be in the "National Enquirer." Keaven finally considered the issue of who was really converting whom in this situation. Maybe retreat was the best course of action, but Keaven was not made for retreating.

14 AWKWARD

Mo was the first to knock on Keaven's door the next day. Opening it, Mo unleashed, "What are you thinking? What were you thinking kissing Chel Colton and having a picture of it shot? I told everybody you were my friend. I've received hundreds, no, thousands, of emails, saying they always knew I was a Democrat. What a disaster. My friend hanging out with the devil of all Democrats, ruining my Republican street cred. forevermore. I have half a mind not to speak to you ever again."

"Slow down, Mo," Keaven commanded. "You know that, if you unfriend me, your number of friends will decline by 50 percent."

Mo started to look away, furtively saying, "You wouldn't hold anything against me if I was helping a mutual friend. Would you?"

"What did you do, Mo?" Keaven commanded. Mo looked away. Keaven again asked, "What did you do, Mo?"

"Tricia called me this morning, distraught at seeing the picture of you kissing Chel and asked for your emails to her," Mo replied. He continued, "I gave them to her and couldn't even believe what you were saying to Chel."

"Mo, how many times have I asked you to stop hacking?" Keaven replied. "Why would you hack me of all students, your best friend?"

Mo countered, "I like Tricia, too. Sometimes friends have to tell friends what they don't want to hear, too. Chel's playing you. You have a gift, but sometimes there's a match or a better person with that gift out there. Cut your losses before you lose Tricia."

Keaven replied, "You know me too well, Mo. I don't give up."

Mo replied, "Though you walk through the valley of death and fear no evil, you are totally off your path. There's nowhere in the Bible that says, 'Go to the devil and change him or her.' Instead, the common message is to stay away from the devil. Live your life without the devil in it."

Keaven calmly responded, "While you are more or less correct, you don't see the opportunity for what it is, to convert the President's daughter to our cause. She's only a moderate Democrat. That's feasible. Moderate Democrat to at least Independent if not fully to Republican."

Mo countered, "At what price? It's a pyrrhic victory. The effort required to turn her would be better spent evangelizing the masses. Even a common everyday California liberal could be converted. You're trying to convert a devil into an angel. God's not even that good."

Mo continued, "After Tricia and I both dealt with your emails to Chel together, I was able to get you one last shot with Tricia, tonight, dinner at 9:00 PM."

Keaven replied, "No, you didn't, Mo."

Mo replied, "What? You should be thanking me for saving your relationship."

"I have plans with Chel tonight at 9:00 PM with which you have to help me," Keaven replied.

Mo countered, "Why does Tricia mean so little to you now? You think you can play with everybody, including me. I thought you were different than the typical Democrat. I was wrong. Maybe you are a

Democrat. How do you like that, Democrat? What would your father, mother, and Rosa say?"

Keaven replied, "That's so unfair of you to say, Mo. I'm doing this for the greater good."

"That's what every Democrat says," Mo replied. "You have to decide whether you are a formalist or a utilitarian. Formalists are Republicans, and utilitarians are Democrats. Choose wisely."

"Give me one more shot at Chel. If I cannot get her to move at all tonight, I'll give up," Keaven countered.

Mo answered, "We both know you won't give up. You have to understand what is changeable and what is not. God, grant me the determination to change what I can. God, grant me the courage to endure what I cannot change. God, grant me the wisdom to know the difference. Do you now understand what I'm saying?"

Keaven replied, "One more night, Mo. Then I'm done for good."

Mo countered, "I say exactly the same thing about hacking, but I continue to do it."

"Just make fake IDs for me and Chel to get in the 21 clubs in town and then find out from your internet brethren the best clubs in the area. I need to make a great second impression to be successful in my quest," Keaven countered.

Mo replied, "You don't even know what you're saying or doing. You're not yourself. Chel has you right in the palm of her hand."

"Come on. Just do it. In exchange, you can ask Tricia out tonight at 9:00 PM," Keaven cajoled.

Mo continued, "Believe me. I don't need your permission

anymore for that. She just wants to be loved. She wants that to be you. If I continue to fill in, you won't be that person anymore. How would that affect all our friendships? Chel is bad news. You know it and just don't want to admit it. I give up, though. Here's a print out of the IDs that I've attached to hard plastic to make them look official and a print out of the best clubs. Try Mezzanine and Ruby Skye."

Keaven replied in astonishment, "Someday you'll have to teach me how you can do all this tech stuff and so quickly."

"It's a gift just like having you as a friend used to be," Mo replied with disgust. He walked out of the room like a man who was walking to his own execution.

Mezzanine and Ruby Skye looked to be the prime choices for the night life. Mezzanine had 12,000 square feet to enjoy the best in DJ beats. Ruby Skye had two levels for DJ entertainment.

The whole situation somehow did not feel right to Keaven. He continued to justify it to himself as a necessary evil to win a powerful ally.

Keaven met Chel at the prearranged point, the entrance to her dorm complex. Evidently, she had snuck away from her handlers.

Chel was breath taking. She was wearing a black tank top, saying "How Grave that I Live to Rave," with jeans. The look was topped off with sunglasses, and she had died her hair purple. Keaven wondered what her father would say to that look.

"Corey Hart always said to watch out for anybody wearing sunglasses at night," Keaven commented.

"I have to find some way of fitting in for once," Chel replied. "Have some compassion for me here."

"I'm not 21. You're not 21. Unfortunately, that means we have to use these fake IDs," Keaven explained with some level of guilt, his conscience starting to get to him.

"You looked 22. I guess I was misled because of how hot you are," Chel continued.

Keaven did not mind hearing the words. However, he was smart enough to realize he was getting played to some extent.

"Mezzanine first for Oakenfold. Then it's Ruby Skye for Tong," Keaven replied. "In case you don't know, they're two of the top DJs in the world."

"I may have lived in prison in the White House, but I was not dead," Chel answered. "I'm impressed. I can tell you know your stuff. My faith definitely was not misplaced."

"I can cover the tab," Keaven explained.

Chel continued, "No, I pay my own way. In fact, I'm covering you tonight for freeing me from the monotony that is my life."

At Mezzanine, Keaven was shocked Chel could dance. She could really dance. "Where'd you pick up the moves?"

Chel shouted through the music and fans, "One of the guys in my detail used to be a dancer at a club."

Keaven replied, "Wouldn't have expected anybody to work in both those fields."

Finally, they were off to Ruby Skye. There, they both had a surprise. Will Colton was there at a VIP table. He waved for Chel and

Keaven to come over and sit with him. "What are you doing here, Dad?" Chel asked.

Will replied, "I could ask you the same thing. I came out for a surprise trip, but Jace and Susana told me you were planning to sneak out tonight. I told them to let you enjoy yourself some but to get me to your final destination for some family time together."

He continued, "Who's the guy?"

Keaven responded, "I'm Keaven Deal."

Will commented, "Somehow, you look familiar. I never forget a face. Somehow, your name seems familiar. I never forget a name either. I'll figure it out. Just give me some time."

Keaven sat between Chel and Will. Will had the entire VIP area filled with a Secret Service detail.

Will asked Keaven above the noise of the music, "So what attracted you to my daughter?"

Keaven replied, "She's an accomplished woman even though she is but 18-years old. Obviously, you have taught her well. She has wisdom far beyond her years and a knowledge of the world but a few individuals have."

Will interrupted, "And she's beautiful, too. Right?"

"Of course," Keaven answered. "That part kind of goes without saying."

Will commented, "I like the music, Chel. How come you never played any of this?"

Keaven interrupted, "Trance music."

Will finished, "Trance music at home?"

"There were always far more important things to talk about than what music I enjoyed listening to," Chel replied.

Will continued with Keaven, "So how did the two of you meet?"

Chel answered for Keaven this time, "At a protest."

Will, looking even more interested, said, "You were protesting my policy, too, on the bombing in Iraq?"

Keaven replied, "Actually, I was supporting your policy."

Will commented, "That stand takes courage for anybody living on the Leftist Coast. Thanks for the support."

Chel commented, "He didn't protest for long because I called the police."

Will replied, "That's my gal."

Somehow this whole situation was turning into the worst of dreams. Keaven fully realized there was no way he could ever turn Chel. She took too much after her father for that transformation ever to happen. Bad dreams surprisingly could become far worse. At that moment, Mo and Tricia walked in. They eventually saw Keaven and had for a moment joy in their faces. However, as they turned to see Chel to his right and Will to his left, their countenances soon turned sour.

Mo looked more disappointed than Keaven had ever seen him. Tricia looked as furious as a hurricane. She came charging toward the table. Somehow, Tricia dodged every Secret Service agent there to get right in front of Keaven, saying, "It's over."

Keaven replied, "What's over? I don't even know who you are."

Tricia countered, "So that's the game? I don't even matter now that you've met the allegedly great Chel so that you can get to the allegedly great Will? Everything makes sense now."

Keaven intoned, "Hey, Mo, come over here and take your girlfriend home."

Tricia slapped him and walked away on her own accord toward Mo, embracing him, and then walking arm and arm with him out the entrance.

"I apologize for that display, Mr. President," Keaven began. "I know the guy, Mo. He's a great computer science student, kid of an Apple executive, but I don't know the girl. Apparently, she thinks she knows me."

Will replied, "Don't worry about it. I've been through similar situations before. You should probably catch your friend, Mo. That way, I can have some family time alone with Chel."

As Keaven walked by, Will whispered in his ear, "Don't worry. I'll smooth things over with Chel. She needs a great guy like you in her life. I am the great communicator after all."

Keaven wanted to say, "No, Will, President Reagan was." However, he did not say it.

Once he was at the entrance, he saw Tricia and Mo on their way to the BART. Keaven ran with all his might but could only get to the door as it closed. He looked at Tricia and Mo through the glass as the BART veered away.

Keaven was left with his thoughts. He now felt like he should like dirt. Keaven had treated Mo and then especially Tricia like dirt. Faced with his accusers, he acted like a Colton, not like a Deal.

His dad and mom would have been ashamed of how he had behaved tonight. He had never lied in his life before. Somehow, in the presence of what he occasionally considered to be evil, Will Colton, he had been transformed into somebody different. He constantly asked himself: "What just happened?"

His ultimate conclusion was that he had been played. Will and Chel Colton were superior to him in playing the game. The implication was that not only had he lost Tricia and possibly Mo, his only friends in this world, but he had also lost belief in his power to change individuals for the better, to generate necessary support for his cause.

Becoming President in an instant had moved from possible to improbable. He began to say to himself, "Why did I choose to come to California? Did I somehow think I could convert the entire state? How did I think anything would be any different than my experience in LA?"

All he could do was pray, "God, save me from myself. Put me back on a productive path. If I am not to be President, somehow find some use for me."

Suddenly, he was surrounded by a local street gang, the 11th Street gang. The gang leader yelled, "Hola, chico. ("Hello, boy.") You're in the wrong place at the wrong time. This is our block. This is our time."

Keaven responded to the ten, all seeming to pack knifes at the least and handguns at the most, "I'm in the right place at the right time."

The gang leader replied, "Are you a cop?"

"If I were a cop, would I come here without a gun, without any back-up?" Keaven replied. "Trust me. We should all get on our ways because the President of the US is in the area tonight. That means cops will be out tonight more than ever."

The gang leader smiled and replied, "Sounds like something somebody would say if they were caught in the wrong place at the wrong time."

"Just remember after this entire situation is over that I warned you," Keaven replied.

The gang leader said, "You know of course that we set out tonight to find a target for two of our initiates to kill to prove themselves worthy of our gang. Suddenly, we found you all alone, waiting for the next BART. It's your unlucky day."

The gang members then drew their guns and knives. The two initiates started walking toward Keaven. He considered his situation: There was good news, and then there was bad news. The good news was that more police would be in the area than ever with President Colton in town. The bad news was that none was around at the immediate moment. The good news was that the two walking toward him had not taken the safeties off their guns, at least not yet. The bad news was that the more experienced gang members, who were surrounding him, had. In the end, though, Keaven had his survival instinct and his father's special forces education in self-defense.

At final count, Keaven faced four handguns and six knives. It was not an impossible situation. The two initiates were standing right in front of him now, just feet away, pointing their guns at his chest. They still had not taken the safeties off. The other gang members had encircled him, except on the back, to be away from the line of fire. Keaven had been taught not to fight and did not believe in fighting. However, he did not have any other options.

Keaven began to line up the angles for the two non-initiates with handguns. Then, he said, "Your initiates still have not taken the safeties off. Let me help them." In an instant, he used each hand to grab the respective weapons from the initiates, taking the safeties off and shooting the guns out of the hands of the two non-initiates. He then grabbed the initiates by their flannel shirt collars, one in each hand, and started spinning them around him as a shield. This shield, particularly their shoes, knocked out four of the knife-wielding gang members. He then slammed the two spinning initiates' heads together, knocking them out.

Now the odds were fair. Keaven against two knife-wielders and two now unarmed gang members. In the melee, though, Keaven took a knife slash to his left arm. In the process, however, he knocked out the two knife-wielders with spinning karate kicks to their faces. He threw one of the unarmed to the ground.

Just as he was about to dispatch of the remaining unarmed gang member, police finally arrived. Worse still, President Colton was driving by. The police quickly arrested the ten gang members with looks of wonderment on their faces at how Keaven had somehow taken down ten of the most dangerous gang in town all on his own. President Colton, with the gang finally in police cars, climbed out of his limousine contrary to his handlers' advice. He said, "I happened to see most of what you just did. That was impressive. I've never served in combat."

Keaven replied, "I know."

President Colton laughed the barb off, continuing, "I've never served in combat, so I don't know how impressed I should really be. However, some of my Secret Service detail have, and you impressed even them."

Keaven wanted to say, "If you were watching all that display, then why didn't you intervene to save me?" However, he did not say it.

Chel saw it, too. She was impressed. She climbed out, saying, "I can speak for myself, Dad. I knew you were impressive from the first time I saw you." She then kissed him on the cheek. She then noticed his arm bleeding, saying, "Oh, my God, your arm is bleeding."

President Colton remarked, "We have somebody capability of administering first aid, but we should get you to a hospital."

"No, thanks," Keaven replied. "I'm just waiting for the BART to get home."

President Colton replied, "I am Commander in Chief. I order you to go to the hospital."

"I'm not in your chain of command. I'm simply an economics student at Cal Berkeley," Keaven replied.

President Colton continued, "That's pretty impressive. I had you tabbed as a special forces soldier on leave. Somebody smart enough for Cal Berkeley with that kind of fighting capability, you're a rare commodity indeed."

"I'd like to think of myself as a person, not a smart bomb," Keaven remarked.

Now with the Secret Service grabbing him by each arm, there was really no way to say no. The press was there to greet them at the front entrance of the nearest hospital. Why would they not? A Secret Service detail made an emergency call for medical treatment. That call would lead to interest in whether the President's life was in danger. Of course, the President played up the situation to the best extent possible, constantly mentioning, "I'm just hear visiting my daughter over winter break and helping anybody I can along the way."

Keaven had really blown this situation. He was now helping evil incarnate score political ratings just like he did as a kid at Arlington Cemetery with a President being so kind as to acknowledge his existence in such a tragic situation.

Keaven fully knew now that he had been played. The Colton's were better than he was without any doubt.

Every media outlet the next day was showing pictures of Keaven, classifying the tale as the President helping somebody who had been stabbed. Of course, nothing was written about what Keaven did to help remove a gang threat in San Francisco. While Keaven acknowledged being unable to challenge the Colton's political force, he had more difficulty acquiescing in his inability to control the press. The Colton's had that power over him, too.

Keaven constantly tried to email Mo. He did not dare try to email Tricia. There was no response from Mo. Well, Keaven had to adapt to the situation. He had learned a powerful lesson but at too great of a cost. The lesson was never try to convert evil. The best anybody could ever do with evil was to box it in or contain it. Evil would always be evil. The cost was the two friendships that mattered the most to him in the world. At the end of the day, though, Keaven was used to being on his own. He was now living alone again as he had virtually every day since his parents had died. There was some message in that situation, too.

Keaven did not answer any of Chel's request for future dates. He had learned his lesson. From that point forward, Keaven devoted himself to his studies. He graduated top of his class.

Knowing that there was nothing left for him in San Francisco or Silicon Valley in general, he took a venture capital job in Boston. Even though he was moving to another liberal bastion, Keaven knew what he was doing. The only good venture capital firms were in the areas of the allegedly greatest universities. Thus, Boston was the best remaining alternative for VC if he did not work where he went to school. There were now too many bad memories in California to justify staying there any longer.

15 BOSTON VC

The first day on the job, Thomas Market taught him the ropes. He began, "You'll be reviewing requests for VC funding. You should remember that we're here to fund companies beyond the start-up seeding stage. That means you have to find actual businesses in operation to pass them forward. We have no interest in seed-stage capital. Seed stage is where the applicant merely has an idea. Ideas are great. They can lead to highly profitable products and companies. However, as it is, only one in ten of companies we fund actually are successful. If we funded seed stage on up, it could well be one in one-hundred. That one that becomes successful has to compensate so well that it pays for the losses on the other nine. There is no way that one could pay for the losses of 99."

Keaven remarked, "I get it, especially because I took a course in VC at Cal Berkeley."

"That's right," Market interjected. "You're the rare bird who flew the coop of Silicon Valley for Boston."

He saw the look of dismay on Keaven's face, so he quickly explained, "You've made the right decision. Working with Harvard grads is far better. It gives you more exposure to biotech and enough tech to make it interesting. Silicon Valley is basically all tech."

Keaven replied, "I know. The biotech side tends to have the higher profitability of the two."

"That's why you've chosen wisely," Market continued, happy to restore a look of confidence to Keaven. He continued, "You do a good job with this work, and soon you will be making the capital investment decisions and serving on boards. It's also a rewarding business. We're contributing to most of the economic growth that occurs in this country. Our country's GDP growth would be nothing if it weren't for start-ups."

Market finished by saying, "Just remember. Sort the wheat from the chaff. Only give us companies that have started and have huge advantages in their markets."

Keaven answered, "It almost seems unfair. It's more that we're only helping the successful companies become more successful and doing nothing to help the above average become great."

Market responded, "In the end here, we have a responsibility to the investors who have contributed to our capital to invest in the VC arena. We have a duty to them and ourselves and no obligation to making companies better in the aggregate. Finally, we're only interested in investing in companies run by Harvard grads or possibly minorities."

"What?" Keaven remarked with surprise, not believing what he had heard.

Market continued, "Most of the investors are from Harvard. We sell them on the idea that they are helping their brothers and sisters in Crimson. You have to understand that, if you attend Harvard, you believe you are the best of best. As such, why would you ever invest on your own in a company run by somebody not from Harvard?"

Keaven challenged, "There are plenty of highly intelligent individuals, who, for one reason or another, choose to attend other private schools and, dare I say it, public schools. What happens to them?"

Market responded, "That's not our concern."

"What about the emphasis on minority-run companies then?" Keaven questioned.

"We're seen as diverse and more socially acceptable if we have a mixture of investment that includes investments in minority-run companies," Market replied.

"Why isn't diversity in investment in terms of area considered?" Keaven replied. "There are really no VC firms in the middle of the country."

Market concluded, "If somebody wanted to build a business worthy of VC, they would have attended school where VC firms exist. It's their fault, not ours or yours, for making poor choices in their lives."

Keaven did not buy what was being sold. However, he was the employee, not the employer. He took the job bent on making so much money as possible. Now that the Colton's had firmly grounded his aspirations of serving as President of the US, becoming the richest possible person seemed to be the only goal left worth pursuing. At least the society in which he found himself living seemed to indicate that goal was the only one worth pursuing.

Time passed. Keaven was good at what he did, receiving promotions and the concomitant increased compensation. Somehow, the money did not seem to matter. It did not buy him happiness. Keaven had experienced a lot of tragedy in his life, yet there had been time for joy. He never knew joy like he had in all too short lived of moments with Rosa, Shadia, Mo, and Tricia. In the end then, Keaven had a rendezvous with his destiny, not theirs. Reagan had his rendezvous with destiny, too. Unfortunately, Keaven's was not the same. It involved money, not leadership or politics.

Soon it was September 11, 2001. It was initially just another day. While stock brokers had access to breaking news, such access was less important to VC firms. However, they did have a television set in the waiting room. VC applicants, who had made it through the vetting process, had to come to the firm for their final pitch. The television set could prove to be a welcome distraction from such an important event in the life of a company, the life of an executive team, and the life of its employees.

Despite promotions, Keaven was still clearing the way by looking through applications. He had learned well from his superiors to discard all applicants involving individuals outside the Harvard program, save for minorities of course. Thankfully enough, those individuals who were minorities had no difficulty making that fact front and center in their applications to make it seem that this particular fact was far more important than the company they had.

Yells and screams started to emanate from the waiting room. Keaven saw individuals running in the hall toward the waiting room. Keaven was well attuned to his job and did not let these distractions deter him.

He suddenly received a call on his phone. He looked at the clock, 8:50 AM Eastern Standard Time. Keaven never seemed to receive calls from anybody, especially before noon. Oh, well, he answered.

"Hello, this is Keaven Deal at . . . ."

A woman's voice interrupted him, "Thank God I reached you. It's Tricia."

"How did you find me, Tricia?" Keaven replied.

"God helped," Tricia responded. Keaven looked at the two pictures on his desk, the one of Mo and Tricia and the one of Tricia kissing Keaven from a Christmas long ago.

Keaven continued, "I tried my best to run away from you. We've never dealt with what happened that night. I want to maintain that detente."

"My time might be short, so let's let bygones be bygones," Tricia indicated.

"What do you mean?" Keaven replied.

"For somebody so perceptive, it surprises me sometimes how you can miss the obvious," Tricia replied. "I work at Cantor Fitzgerald, top floors of World Trade Center, the North Tower. A plane just crashed into the tower."

Because Keaven liked to watch the Red Sox play, he had snuck a television set into his office and cabled it to the set in the waiting room. It was a trick Mo had taught him long ago. Keaven worked late nights, and he wanted to watch the Red Sox. No further explanation was necessary.

He turned on a major news network. He saw the replay of the airliner crashing into the tower. Keaven said, "That's not a plane. That's a commercial airliner. What are you doing talking to me? Get out of the tower."

Tricia replied, "I can't. Others tried to get down, but the way is blocked by fire and plane debris. I'm trapped."

"Get off the phone and look for a way out," Keaven implored.

"I'm on a cell phone, so I've already looked at every possible way of escape. There's none," Tricia plaintively replied.

As they were showing a live look at Tricia's tower, suddenly another airliner entered the picture and crashed into the South Tower.

Keaven heard the boom over the phone, the screams from Tricia's tower, and the screams from the waiting room.

"Oh, my God, what just happened?" Tricia asked.

"Another commercial airliner crashed into the South Tower," Keaven replied. "This whole situation is no accident. How many minutes of battery power do you have on the cell phone?"

Tricia replied, "I don't know."

Keaven countered, "Grab at least one more cell phone from an office, and get to the roof or at least the top floor. Continue to talk to me even though I may not be able to respond every moment." Keaven grabbed a jewelry box from his top drawer and ran to Market's office.

Keaven told Thomas Market, "I'm off to NYC on a Flexitjetit Learjet."

"What?" Market commanded, "They've grounded all commercial flights. They wouldn't let you take off even if you had an appointment. It's $50,000 for each flight."

Keaven implored, "Please get it set up for me. Flexitjetit is one of our investments. I'll pay you back. I have a significant other trapped in the World Trade Center. Time matters. I'm on my way, counting on you getting it set up by the time I'm at the plane."

"All right," Market relented. "Who do you think you are? You're not a fireman."

Keaven was on his way before he could react to that statement. As he was racing down the stairs, not taking a chance on the elevator not working, Tricia talked to him, "What are you doing?"

Keaven talked while running, "I'm taking a flight to NYC where I will get a helicopter to take me to the top floors of your tower. Once up there, by rope or any means possible, I'll save you." He was now at ground level out of breath, hailing a cab.

Tricia complained, "You heard what he said. They've grounded all commercial flights. They're only allowing military jets in the skies."

Keaven climbed in the cab and shouted the directions to the private airfield, saying he'd pay $1,000 for the fastest the driver could get him there. "At some time in your life, you believed in me. I ask you to believe in me again. I've lost far too many people I love, and I'm not going to lose you."

Tricia ventured, "You have to accept that there is a chance I'm not going to be able to survive this situation. We have to make our peace while we can."

"I'm not giving up. You're the most important thing I've had in my life since my parents died," Keaven shared, tears filling his eyes.

"This is really unfair of me to say, but I wish you would have told me those words even once in San Francisco. If you had, I probably wouldn't be in this situation," Tricia continued.

"There was no going back once you saw me with Chel and President Colton," Keaven replied.

"Why did Mo ever bring you there?" Keaven questioned. "Some friend, he turned out to be."

The cabdriver reached the field in record time. Keaven threw him ten $100 bills and raced for a fueling jet. Tricia began to talk, but Keaven interrupted, "Save it for until I get in the plane. I won't hear what you say otherwise."

The fueling jet turned out not to be his. Keaven somehow convinced the pilot that it was. The pilot indicated, "We're grounded. The FAA has cancelled all non-military flights."

Keaven asked, "Does this plane have autopilot?"

The pilot responded, "Yes, but not for take-off and landing."

Keaven questioned, "Is the insurance policy paid up?"

The pilot replied with concern in his voice, "Yes, but I'm not taking this plane up against a threat of being shot down by military jets."

"Don't worry. I'll take it up myself," Keaven responded.

"Have you ever flown before?" the pilot countered.

"Everybody always has a first time," Keaven replied.

The pilot shouted, "This is my plane, my responsibility, and it's not taking to the skies today."

Keaven tripped him to the floor of the plane, pulled him out of the plane onto the tarmac, closed the door, and ran to the cockpit. He located the autopilot, quickly read the flight manual, and said to himself, "This is far safer than what the Wright Brothers did."

He had played enough flight simulator to know about take-offs, but he always seemed to have problems with the landings. Oh, well, there was always the first time for a successful landing, too, flight simulator or for real.

Keaven told Tricia, "You can continue now."

Tricia replied, "What did you do to the pilot?"

"Don't worry about it. He's still alive," Keaven countered.

As Keaven generated enough pace for take-off, Tricia continued, "Mo brought me there to help convince me to give you another chance. He was nothing but a great friend to you. I wanted to cut you loose based on the emails and the picture of you kissing her. That stuff was really low of you. Your kisses at the club drove the final nail in the coffin. I'd never known hurt like that in my life."

Keaven replied, "That's because you've never lost any of your parents like I did. All I've known my entire life seems to be hurt."

A voice suddenly came over the radio, getting Keaven's immediate attention. "This is flight leader, Cuba Libre. Descend to 10,000 feet and turn southward to return to the airport from which you have just taken off."

Keaven replied, "This is Keaven Deal, and I'm on an important rescue mission."

"Captain Deal, our orders are to escort you back to the ground or shoot you down. There's no wiggle room," Cuba Libre responded.

"Look, Cuba Libre. You're only alive today because I helped save you and your mother from the Straits of Florida a decade or so ago.

Do me this small favor and escort me to NYC," Keaven commanded.

Cuba Libre suddenly remembered. "How did you know it was me?" Cuba Libre asked.

"That doesn't matter now. I'm trying to save another life. Just tell your superiors that I have landing gear issues and am trying to find a save spot to land. That tale will buy us some time," Keaven relayed.

Cuba Libre replied, "I'm not alone up here. There are others."

"That's true. There are a lot of angels up there, but, for right now, I just need you," Keaven commanded.

"Your turn, Tricia, to continue talking," Keaven replied.

"Why did you treat me like dirt? I loved you," Tricia continued.

Keaven responded:

I was trying to do something for the greater good. I learned, though, that there was no changing Chel. I also learned that I'd never be President because I couldn't defeat Will at any turn. He played me like a puppet just as Chel did. Like father, like daughter.

"Typical of a politician, you didn't answer the question," Tricia responded.

Keaven continued, "You know after Rosa that I never wanted to allow anybody to get close to me again until you entered my life. I couldn't handle the hurt. Without somebody in my life, I felt untouchable. With somebody in my life, I was not untouchable. I had to worry about your safety."

Tricia continued, "You cared so much about my safety that you never contacted me again."

"I know. It sounds like I didn't care, but everybody who gets close to me somehow experiences misfortune," Keaven continued.

Cuba Libre interjected, "That's not true. I'm fine."

"So far, Cuba Libre, so far," Keaven replied. "This conversation was kind of meant to be private."

Cuba Libre intervened, "You know the flight time from Boston to New York City is about 39 minutes. You're almost there, ten minutes out, but we have trouble up here. Two commercial airliners have veered off course, vectoring toward DC. Another fighter will take over, making you land or shoot you down before you get close to NYC. I bought you so much time as I could, but there are lives at stake here that I have to secure. Do you understand?"

"God bless, you, Cuba Libre," Keaven replied.

"God bless, you, Keaven, and thank you again for saving my life," Cuba Libre commented, turning his jet supersonic toward the South. The sonic boom left a strong reminder of the power of an American fighter.

"Somebody just said that a plane crashed in DC," Tricia replied, starting to cry.

"Stay strong, Tricia," Keaven implored. "You're a MacDiller. You're a soldier's daughter."

"But the world's falling apart," Tricia countered.

"Learjet, Captain Deal, this is Leatherneck," the new fighter pilot broke over the radio.

"This is Captain Deal. I'm en route to NYC, seeking a safe landing place due to landing gear malfunction," Keaven replied.

"There's no way I'm letting you land anywhere near NYC, Captain Deal," Leatherneck continued. "You land at any small airport or even on a highway but do not progress any farther toward NYC."

Keaven countered, "Leatherneck, you're a marine pilot. You went through hell to get to flight school unlike the air force fighter jocks. Right?"

Leatherneck replied, "Yes, sir."

"Do I sound like a terrorist, Leatherneck, after I have correctly identified you as a marine pilot and made you aware that I know the hell you had to climb out of to get to where you are now?" Keaven asked.

"No, sir, but . . .," Leatherneck continued.

Keaven interrupted, "I want you to introduce you to Tricia. She is calling from the World Trade Center. Say hi, Tricia."

"Hi, Leatherneck," Tricia communicated.

"You know the World Trade Center that is on fire with all her escapes blocked. Her father is special forces at MacDill. My father was special forces at MacDill. My father died in the Battle of Mogadishu," Keaven continued. "Do we sound like terrorists to you? I'm on a mission to save her life."

Leatherneck commented, "You know orders better than anybody then."

"Do you love anybody, Leatherneck?" Keaven continued.

Leatherneck responded, "Yes, I do."

"What would you do if you were trying to save that person's life and a fighter pilot told you that he would stop you because of his orders?" Keaven asked.

"I'd ignore him because there's the chance he might not shoot you down," Leatherneck replied.

"Air Command, I'm escorting Learjet to the nearest possibility landing point. No additional fighter support is required," Leatherneck relayed to ground control.

Tricia said, "Thank you."

Leatherneck replied, "You know I'm risking my career for this."

"If we somehow pull this off, I will give you my father's Medal of Honor and defend you for the rest of your life from any possible repercussions," Keaven replied.

"Not necessary, sir," Leatherneck replied. "While I'm up here, nobody will touch you."

Tricia continued, "How do you do it, Keaven?"

"If you're honest with individuals and tell them what's at stake, they usually make the right decision. If you lie, you're done before you start," Keaven responded.

Tricia questioned, "So that's what you learned from the Chel situation?"

"It was a lesson at too great of a cost, losing the only two friends I had in California," Keaven continued.

"Leatherneck, my flight plan is to crash land in the Hudson or find a spot on Governors Island," Keaven interjected. "I need you to requisition a helicopter be fueled ready for take-off at Heli Flight Services—Heli Tours."

"Today of all days, a civilian helicopter crew will listen to a fighter pilot on a rescue mission," Keaven continued.

"All flights are grounded, including helicopters, especially in NYC under FAA orders," Leatherneck responded.

"Just remember all that you've been through to get where you are and the fact that I will fight for you the rest of your life to help me save this life," Keaven replied.

"You're asking a lot," Leatherneck replied.

Keaven continued: "A person's life is worth more than a person's career, Leatherneck. Making the wrong choice is something that haunts you for the rest of your life. I know it all too well."

"Heli Flight Services—Heli Tours, this is Leatherneck, F-15 fighter pilot en route to NYC on rescue mission, requesting a helicopter be fueled and ready for take-off in minutes," Leatherneck demanded. "Understood. Thank you for your cooperation with the military."

Leatherneck replied, "Done and done, Captain Deal. Two minutes out. I'm climbing to 40,000 feet, vectoring over NYC. Good luck to you, both."

Keaven responded, "Good luck, Leatherneck. You're a hero." Soon, another supersonic boom greeted Keaven as Leatherneck jetted away.

Then Keaven heard more screaming over the phone and Tricia, saying, "Oh, my God, the Second Tower just collapsed. It was hit second, and it just collapsed."

Keaven knew that meant time was even shorter than he had

hoped. Tricia opined, "Why do we take life for granted? It's such a dream. We have everything, but we don't realize it until it's too late."

"If I have to take this plane, this helicopter, and whatever else through hell, I'll do it for you," Keaven implored. "Don't ever give up. Believe in me."

Keaven continued, "I've been carrying this cell phone a long time, so my battery could run out. Don't give up hope, especially if you don't hear me back. Also, I'll be landing the plane, which will be a difficult thing for me."

"Why are you doing all this for me?" Tricia replied.

"Because I love you," Keaven responded.

"I love you, so why are we not together?" Tricia questioned.

"We always were. I never stopped thinking about you," Keaven continued.

Tricia replied, "If we only had said these things earlier, we wouldn't be in this situation."

Keaven found enough space to try to land on Earlybird Road on Governors Island, which was about so close as he could get to the helicopter.

"Still there, Tricia?" Keaven asked, running to the helicopter.

Tricia continued, "Yes, you should know something I didn't want to tell you before. The fire and the heat are so great that don't be surprised as you see some from this building jumping to their deaths. It's heart breaking and unbearable, but you have to be prepared for it."

The helicopter pilot did not question whether he could take to the skies after Leatherneck's seemingly authoritative orders, saving time. In minutes, the helicopter was near the tower. The problem was that the smoke emanating from the building made rescue virtually impossible.

"Tricia, I want you to guide us toward you by whether the sound of the helicopter is getting closer or farther away from you. Do you understand?" Keaven asked.

"Yes," Tricia continued.

The pilot replied, "I can't take it down any closer. I can't see through the smoke. It's too dangerous."

"We're wasting critical time," Keaven replied. "If we approach from the other side, the wind won't push the smoke toward us."

"All right," the pilot replied. A flight controller broker over the radio, "Helicopter, you are to return to your launching point. Flights over NYC are forbidden by FAA order."

"It's 10:25 AM. Give me four more minutes before you acknowledge that return-to-base order," Keaven replied. "Leatherneck told you this was a rescue mission. Didn't he?"

"Fine," the pilot responded.

"I'm going to open the door, stand on the landing gear, and extend this rope that you thankfully found on short notice before we took off so far as I can," Keaven commanded.

"Tricia, you be looking for that rope," Keaven demanded over the phone.

"What if others try to grab it before me?" Tricia replied.

Keaven replied, "I'll try to save so many as we can each trip at a time, but you are first without any argument. If it means fighting over the rope, you have to do it. I can't live without you. If you believe in what I can accomplish, then you have to live, if not for you, then for the country."

"It's 10:27, and we haven't seen her yet," the pilot intoned.

"Yes, we have," Keaven replied. "She's there." He suddenly saw Tricia's face through the smoke as if a miracle were about to occur. "Get me there," he implored.

Keaven extended the rope, saw her face, and watched her mouth the words, "I love you." Just as she was about to grab the rope, the tower collapsed. His watch said 10:28 and 22 seconds. It was a time that Keaven would remember for the rest of his life. His head fell to his chest in grief. The pilot had to yell at him several times to get back in the helicopter before Keaven noticed.

The pilot then intervened, "I'm sorry. My God, I'm sorry. I tried to do everything I could."

Back in his seat, Keaven looked up, saying, "You did everything you could. She died because I couldn't appreciate, love, what I had, the most beautiful of souls on earth." All Keaven could do was shake his head and let tears fall down his face.

"I'm returning to the helipad. Is that all right?" the pilot asked.

Keaven replied, "There's nothing more that we can do here for anybody now that the two towers have collapsed."

The pilot commented as they flew away from the scene, "She sounded like a really special person."

Keaven commented, "She was a one in a million. The one person on this earth who was my soulmate. She was worth more than all the money and power in the world. Tricia was literally an angel."

The pilot replied, "While you might not have said to her everything you wanted, she knew you loved her."

"What do you mean?" Keaven questioned.

"You landed a private plane almost into the ground on Governors Island just in an attempt to save her, risking your own life," the pilot intoned.

"It's not the half of it," Keaven commented.

The pilot continued, "Words are words. Deeds are deeds. There is no more powerful act of love than risking your own life to save another. She knew."

"I appreciate it," Keaven genuinely intoned. "By the way, what's your name?"

"I'm Matteo Martin, sir," he replied.

"I'll never forget you, Matteo, because you gave me a chance to try to save her and a chance to see her one last time," Keaven replied. "Are you planning on proposing to a girl any time soon?"

"Yes, but I don't have enough money for a ring," Matteo replied.

"Here's a ring," Keaven, taking the ring meant for Tricia out of his pocket and putting it on Matteo's lap.

Keaven intoned, "What today should teach us is that tomorrow's not guaranteed. Don't make love wait another day. You have a ring now, so you have no more excuses."

"I can't," Matteo replied.

"You can," Keaven responded. "What's her name?"

"Tricia," Matteo replied.

A tear formed in his eye again. Keaven replied, "Some things were just meant to be."

Because of worries about repetition of the events of that day, the fact that Keaven had flown a Learjet and been in a helicopter around NYC during a time all flights were supposed to be grounded was kept from the public. Keaven's and Matteo's heroics were never mentioned in the annals of 9/11. Cuba Libre and Leatherneck survived their transgressions by relying on the fact that Keaven had told them his landing gear did not work. Matteo was never reprimanded for his flight in part because it would have brought to light questions about why the available helicopters were not better employed in a rescue.

So great was his sadness at losing Tricia, Keaven could not attend her funeral. He could not face her family but wrote this message to them: "Tricia was the most beautiful of souls ever to be on this earth. She made this world a better place. I loved her more than I ever loved anything, save for my dad and mom. This world is a much darker place today without her. I don't know how I will be able to go on. As I dated her at Berkeley with a ring in hand, I didn't do the right thing and propose to her the first chance I had. I let ambition get in the way of love. I have so much guilt in my heart for not finding a way to save her. While I cannot bring her back, I will find the person who orchestrated the attack. Once he has been brought to justice, my reason for being on this earth will be at an end. Catching the killer and getting to Heaven to be with Tricia and my parents are the only things I have left."

16 9/12

The next day, Keaven withdrew enough money from his bank account to pay off the debts he incurred the previous day. Once he completed these money transfers, Keaven typed a resignation letter to Market and left it on his desk.

His next step was to venture to the Boston army recruiter to sign up for military service. The recruiter's name was Terence Miller, Jr. It seemed familiar to Keaven. He was about to sign the enlistment contract but decided to ask Terence whether he was related to Terence, Sr., the soldier who had served with Keaven's father. In seconds, fate started to unfold. Terence, Jr., was Terence, Sr.'s, son. Soon enough, Keaven was on the phone speaking with Terence, Sr.

Terence, Sr., began, "So you're signing up for the military now? What took you so long?"

Keaven replied, "I apologize. After I lost Dad and Mom, I went through a series of unfortunate events that ultimately led to me studying economics at Cal Berkeley. I had a job at a Boston VC. Then, 9/11 happened."

Terence, Sr., questioned, "What's the real reason you're signing up?"

"What do you mean?" Keaven asked.

Terence, Sr., continued, "It's like you said before. You chose to attend college before enlisting, so there must be some reason all of a sudden you're signing up."

Keaven, growing angry even though he was among good company, replied, "If you want to know, I flew a private jet to NYC from Boston, averted two military jets, requisitioned a helicopter, and came within seconds of saving the woman I wanted to marry from falling to her death in the North Tower. I want to find the leader responsible for the plan and kill . . . I mean bring him to justice."

"No good," Terence, Sr., responded. "You're not in the right state of mind to make this decision."

"You have to be kidding me," Keaven replied. "We're virtually family. I have been taught how to be a killing machine. I want vengeance."

"That's proof you're not of the right mind to make this decision," Terence, Sr., replied. "Get Jr. back on the phone."

Keaven followed orders. Sr. evidently told Jr. to put the phone on speakerphone so that everybody could hear the rest of the conversation.

Sr. continued, "Jr., don't let Keaven enlist with you or anybody else. Send an email to the Department of Defense, asking them to deny Keaven Deal enlistment under my order. Now that I'm the leader of special forces, my order will have enough weight to ensure he's not allowed to enlist."

Keaven yelled, "Why are you doing this to me? You know I'll be a better soldier than anybody the army signs today and in following days."

Sr. replied, "You said it yourself. You went to Berkeley and studied. Your parents told me how brilliant and special you were. Everybody has their place. Yours is not to die among the enlisted but instead to live to lead."

Keaven said, "Both of you mean a lot to me because of your connection to my father. I have to respect your decision, but keep in mind that there's always the CIA, NSA, and other organizations. My vengeance will happen some way or another."

Sr. intoned, "Don't run away just yet, Keaven. Jr., keep him there because I want him to talk with Matt. If I don't get the chance to communicate again with you at least any time soon, Keaven, just know that I'm doing this in your best interests out of devotion to your father's request to look out for you."

What could Keaven say? He replied, "Thanks, sir."

Jr., knowing family friend, Matt Holmes, quickly had him on speakerphone.

Jr. answered, "Hi, Matt, this is Terence, Jr. Sr. wanted me to have you talk with Keaven Deal. You remember him. Don't you?"

Matt replied, "Of course, I do. His father helped save my life."

Jr. continued, "Sr. told Keaven that he was not going to be allowed to enlist in the army or any other branch of the military and had me email the DoD to ensure that fact. Keaven's not in the right frame of mind to make any decisions, seeking vengeance for his girlfriend's death yesterday at North Tower. He told my father he will try to join the civilian intelligence community, so you understand why you're on the phone."

Matt responded, "Of course, I understand. Take it off speakerphone and give him the receiver so that I can talk with him privately."

"I work at the CIA now," he began, continuing, "It's because of the injuries I sustained during the Battle of Mogadishu. I had to get a desk job and did not want to be stuck somewhere in the military where a desk job ends your career. I wanted to get vengeance, too. However, it took me a while to get into the CIA because their psychological screening said this vengeance thing was a red flag. Until I could get my house in order at least mentally, they were not letting me in."

Keaven implored, "You know me. You know I can do a good job. You need me."

Matt replied, "I'll make you a deal. You'll never get in the civilian intelligence field with a vengeance attitude."

Keaven replied, "I can hide it. I can give other reasons."

"Our HR is the best in the world because it has to be," Matt replied. "They find out everything, and you stand no chance."

Matt continued, "Here's the deal, Keaven. If you get a JD, you will have enough time away from this event to heal and pass the psychological screening. The JD is the most valuable degree you can have for intelligence work. The CIA has more attorneys than the largest corporations on earth. We stay within the legal rules in everything we do. For instance, we transfer subjects to countries where certain interrogation techniques are legal but necessary to get answers."

Keaven countered, "I want to be a field agent, not an attorney, Matt. I want to get the guy who killed the person who meant the most to me since my parents."

"Your quickest way to the front lines is through a job as an attorney at an international firm," Matt replied. "Then you have a cover for why you are traveling to each country to which you may have to travel."

Keaven replied, "The degree takes years. They'll catch him by then."

Matt countered, "Not likely because he's off the radar in Afghanistan, Iran, Pakistan, or maybe even a former Soviet republic by now. Furthermore, we have a mole at the CIA. There's somebody feeding intelligence information to Russia. While it's very likely Russia was not involved in 9/11, that mole is compromising the security of our field agents, guys like you. They could take you out before you even get a chance to look for him."

Keaven countered, "I'm not scared of anything anymore."

Matt continued: "The deal is the deal. You show me the JD. I'll get you in the CIA off the books. You'll never be official. That way, no mole can sell you out."

Keaven countered, "If you can get me in without the screening, why can't you get me in now off the books?"

Matt replied, "I believe in the reason for the screenings. We can't afford any mistakes in catching the person responsible for 9/11. That person has to be brought to justice to show the world that we will catch anybody who even thinks of doing this type of thing again to deter others from attacking us. With your current mental state, that I assure you from my own experience will remain this way for some time, I'm not prepared for the civilian intelligence community to let you in."

"So that's the deal?" Keaven replied. "Can I trust your word, or do I need to get it in writing?"

"Work on your Arabic, but you can trust my word," Matt replied.

Keaven explained, "With regard to the Arabic, I already know it from high school studies with Shadia Kelani. With regard to trusting your word, I can now tell you that, contrary to what you might expect would delay my appearance in front of you by four years, I will be talking with you in less than two. I took the admission test at Berkeley just in case an economics degree wouldn't get me a job. I scored 99th percentile. I applied to every good school in the country and was admitted. Many wouldn't allow me to defer admission, but one did this long, a good safe school, the University of Illinois Urbana-Champaign. What's more is that they offered me a full-ride academic and books scholarship to try to get me to enroll long ago. It's still on the table. Despite normal accreditation rules, requiring an extra year, I have a two-year graduation plan on the table that I can and will execute."

"Somehow, none of these facts seems surprising given how great your father was and how special he told me you were," Matt countered. "If Urbana-Champaign is the destination, the land of Lincoln, then I ask but one more favor of you: Say hello to Dana Denney for me."

"If becoming the best attorney on the face of the planet is the requirement to be able to catch this idiot, then be assured that I will," Keaven replied.

"The last advice I'll give you is to specialize in tax," Matt replied.

"From our agents who have followed the legal callings, I have always heard this joke: Tax attorneys are the least interesting type of attorney to talk with at parties. That also makes them the least likely to seem like an intelligence agent."

"Tax it is then," Keaven responded. "I will be in contact with you again in a little less than two years."

Keaven easily convinced the U. of Illinois to admit him even though he was starting a little late in the semester. They assured him of the two-year plan. They were thrilled just to be able to use his stellar admission score and grade point average to help hike their standing in the legal rankings.

17 DANA DENNEY

Keaven never had read so much in his life. There was a reason years were required to achieve this degree. There were countless hours of reading for every hour spent in class. It left little time for making friends. However, Keaven had learned at this point that having friends only seemed to lead to tragedy. Thus, he was fine with his new life without a life.

Keaven eventually found the time, though, to seek out Dana Denney according to Matt's instructions. His background search, techniques he had learned from Mo through the years, led him to discover she was a local church pastor. Keaven wondered why Matt knew her first of all and wondered second of all why Matt would want him to get in contact with her.

Dana had a special worship group on campus in addition to her regular congregation at church. Keaven decided to try to meet with her on neutral ground at a fruit drink shop.

According to her email response, Dana was willing to meet. Keaven did not order anything but bottled water. Dana made the same choice.

Keaven began, "Why would Matt want me to meet with you? How are the two of you connected?"

Dana replied, "I was a military chaplain assigned to the special forces at MacDill after the Battle of Mogadishu to help soldiers cope with the loss of their comrades. I met Matt there and helped him work through his vengeance issues to get him to the point where he could pass the psychological screenings for the CIA."

Keaven had his two questions answered. Dana was there to help him prepare for life after tragedy.

Dana continued, "It's not even the full answer, though. I was your mother's roommate at Liberty University. We both found a calling in ministry, hers outside the military but mine inside it. Your mom and I communicated regularly during her life. I volunteered for the special counseling at MacDill, knowing she was there. Because of her health issues, though, I tried not to burden you or her. As a result, I never had a chance to meet you formally before now. I say formally because I have been praying for you since your family passed away. In doing so, I feel some informal connection to you already."

"If you're here to check on my mental state, it's fine. We both can just go on our separate ways once you report that fact to Matt," Keaven replied.

"I may have known your mother, but I'll not be cutting you any breaks," Dana replied.

"All right, so you probably want to know about all the crying I've done," Keaven questioned.

"Let me help you answer the question," Dana countered. "Matt filled me in that your girlfriend died in 9/11, so you want me to feel sorry for you probably. I don't."

"What?" Keaven questioned.

"I will not let you be so selfish as to feel sorry for yourself," Dana continued. "Almost 3,000 died, and 6,000 were injured because of September 11's events. You are not injured, and you are alive. You don't deserve anybody to feel sorry for you."

"Are you kidding me?" Keaven replied with surprise. "I lost the love of my life, the only reason I have for living."

"You are acting like this world was created to serve you, to let you be happy each day of your life," Dana continued. "That's not the way it works."

"I suppose I should have committed suicide then," Keaven countered.

"That's a really intelligent answer, not," Dana replied. "You don't understand that God has given each one of us a gift, a reason for existence. You've been given more than just a simple gift. You've been given a great gift."

Keaven replied, "It sounds like you've been talking to God."

"Of course I've been talking with God," Dana answered. "I pray every day."

Allowing a little smile to appear on his face, Keaven said, "I meant God, my friend Mo's online name. At least he used to be my friend, and he would always say that I was meant for something special. Others have, too, mentioning things like next President or governor." Suddenly, Keaven's visage turned somber, saying, "Tricia believed in that power, too."

"When's the last time you talked to God?" Dana asked.

"Which one?" Keaven questioned.

"Either," Dana responded.

"I haven't talked to Mo since he and Tricia caught me dating Chel Colton almost half a decade ago now," Keaven replied. "I've had difficulty talking with the other God since my two parents were killed, since Rosa was killed, and especially now since Tricia was killed."

"So you blame God for your problems or at least for not intervening?" Dana asked.

"What do you think?" Keaven replied.

"Again, that's not how it works," Dana replied. "We converse with God in our time. He responds in his."

"It's not that I don't believe in God. I have to believe in God. If I didn't, why would I still be living? I have to believe that I will someday get to see my parents and Tricia again. It's the only reason I haven't ended my life," Keaven continued.

"Again, you're being so selfish," Dana countered. "You told me that you have some sort of special gift. Guess what? It's not yours. Everything you have is a gift from God. It's not yours. You have an obligation to use your gifts to help others. The parable of the talents tells us this fact."

"I know the parable. Five talents used to produce five more. Two talents used to produce two more. However, the one with but one talent buried at, yielding nothing," Keaven countered.

"I expected as much from somebody raised in your mom's household," Dana replied.

"Look. I've memorized the entire Bible," Keaven replied.

"That's a neat party trick, but it's one thing to memorize. It's an entirely different thing truly to understand," Dana countered.

"Why are you being so tough on me?" Keaven countered.

"It's called tough love," Dana said, continuing, "Right now, you act as if you were entitled to something, some compensation for all the suffering you've endured. Guess what? You're not. There are individuals enduring far greater tragedies and obstacles to success than you are, but they're not here crying about yesterday. They're working and praying for tomorrow."

"I give up trying to get you to feel sorry for me," Keaven continued. "However, how do I move on from all this?"

"It's really quite simple," Dana countered. "First, you have to forgive those who took the lives of those most important to you. Second, you have to forgive yourself because you were not responsible for any of those tragedies."

Keaven replied with indignity, "You want me to forgive the murderer who planned an operation to kill 3,000, including the only person who seemed to matter in my life?"

"The Nazis tried to bomb England into surrender during the Battle of Britain in World War II," Dana intoned, continuing, "They didn't stop, and nothing was free from attack. A church in Coventry was bombed. There's a famous picture of what the congregation next did. In the midst of the rubble, a holy shrine bombed to extinction, the congregation had written 'Father, Forgive' on the altar."

Tears started to form in Dana's eyes as she shared the tale. Keaven thought that maybe she was not that tough after all.

She continued, "If they can forgive, you can forgive. Forgiveness is not for the benefit of the sinner. It's for your benefit so that you can heal and move on."

Keaven intoned, "I forgive."

"Sorry. It's not that easy," Dana countered.

"What do you mean? I said I forgive," Keaven continued.

Dana responded, "You have to believe the words you're saying. Right now, it's obvious you don't. You also have the second task of forgiving yourself that I mentioned."

"I forgive myself," Keaven replied.

"Do you think this whole thing is a game?" Dana chirped.

Keaven said, "The simple fact is that, if I had not become involved in trying to save Rosa, she'd still be alive. If I had been willing to overcome the embarrassment of being caught with Chel and told Tricia how I really felt, she would not have been in NYC on 9/11. She'd still be alive. We'd be married. We'd be happy. My mistakes led to two deaths."

Dana asked, "How did Rosa die?"

Keaven answered, "She was getting abused. I told her I would take her to safety. However, the safety ended up to be the least safe place possible as my stepfather returned her to her abuser. She either was murdered or committed suicide the next day. If not for me, she'd still be alive."

Dana countered, "So you were the one who most directly killed Rosa and Tricia?"

"No, I obviously did not kill Rosa or Tricia directly, but I might as well have for how little good I was to either of them," Keaven responded.

Dana replied, "They each made a choice to get to know you. Rosa ultimately made a choice to follow you to what you both believed was safety. Tricia made her own choice to work in NYC. If you had never existed, Rosa could still have been killed by her abuser or committed suicide. If you had never existed, Tricia very well could have still chosen to work in NYC. Now do you see what I mean about you being selfish, seeing the world as if it only revolved around you?"

Keaven answered, "I guess I understand what you mean. It's difficult to say and don't really know that I can say it."

Dana responded, "You're lucky because you have the aptitude and capability to say a lot of things."

Keaven continued, "I, for the first time, forgive myself, free myself of the guilt, associated with Rosa's and Tricia's deaths."

"You know what, Keaven," Dana continued. "I believe you."

Tears started to form in his eyes after Dana made those comments. Keaven felt a great weight off his shoulders. Keaven continued, "Please give me another chance with forgiving their attackers. You may not like my approach to it, but here it is: Rosa's foster dad, you hurt Rosa and, in so doing me, somebody who cared greatly about her. For how good of a person Rosa was, never wanting others to suffer, she would have wanted me to find some way to forgive you, too, so I do. I forgive you for what you did to her, no matter how abominable. None more difficult words I have ever said. I say them to allow her to rest in peace insomuch as to give myself peace, too, finally. As to Tricia then, for how difficult it was to say goodbye to Rosa, it is just that much more difficult to say goodbye to you not for any other reason than how much more time God gave me to live in your presence. That extra time just makes it all the more painful emotionally. Unfortunately, I knew you all too well. Like Rosa, you never would want to see me suffer. You would want me to move on. To do so requires, though, such a painful thing, forgiving somebody who took the most important person in my life away from me. I forgive you, Osama bin Laden, for ordering the attack."

Keaven somehow believed in the words he had said. Somehow, great weights did seem lifted from his shoulders.

Dana hugged him, saying, "I'm proud of you. Your mom would be proud of you, too. Someday, you'll see them all in Heaven again, but you have an obligation to use your gifts from God to better this world before that happens."

Keaven appreciated the hug. It almost seemed like God himself was hugging him through Dana's arms.

Dana replied, "I ask but one small favor of you."

Keaven did not like to hear those words. The same conversation with Matt had led to him having to meet Dana. In the end, all was well that ended well. He had been made the better for enduring what he just had.

Keaven asked, "What?"

Dana continued, "There is a member of my congregation, Jerome, whose parents died in drug overdoses. He's hearing impaired, but he's somehow found his way through college with help from tutors and disability services. At the end of the day, though, he cannot get a job or a date. He's so down. He questions his faith. I've done what I can, but he needs a big brother. There's nobody who could help him more than you could."

Keaven mentioned, "I'll meet with him here the same place and same time tomorrow. You didn't ask, but I in fact do know sign language."

Dana commented, "I know. Your mother studied it to make her be able to reach more individuals, so I knew you would know it, too. As one last morsel of wisdom, don't waste the years you have in Urbana-Champaign while biding your time before pursuing the terrorist who orchestrated 9/11. There are a lot of special individuals around. Life moves too quickly to squander any opportunity that you're given, especially if you have important gifts to share."

"Thank you for those words and what you've done for me already," Keaven answered.

Dana walked on her way back to her church. Keaven walked on his way back to studying.

18 MEETING JEROME

"Dana tells me that you've accomplished some incredible things, but life is not quite breaking your way these days," Keaven began, signing it and saying it as he would each time he communicated with Jerome.

Jerome replied, signing and saying it as he, too, would during all their conversations, "I'm not good for anything. I apply for every job available, get to the interview, and never get the job. To try to get some confidence, I put a dating profile up for all Illinois. Of the millions of women in Illinois, not one was interested."

Keaven asked, "Did you put that you were hearing impaired in the profile?"

"Of course I did because I want somebody to love me for me," Jerome answered.

"You did the right thing," Keaven countered. "Everybody deserves to have love in their life. Sometimes, though, it just takes time."

"What do you know? Are you dating anybody right now?" Jerome countered.

Keaven was a little taken aback. It still was difficult to talk about Tricia. "I have dated at least one wonderful woman for a long period of time and hung out with some other girls, too. Like a big brother can and should, I can help you out."

"Are you dating anybody right now?" Jerome continued.

"No, I'm not because my studies take all my personal time. I'm trying to graduate in two years with a degree that generally requires an extra year," Keaven countered.

"At least you're being honest with me," Jerome replied.

Keaven was not sure how to react to that comment. He continued, "The priority really should be getting a job and then considering dating. I believe in you and believe both are possible."

Jerome said, "I doubt either is possible and wish I had enough money to get cochlear implant surgery. Then, I could hear."

Keaven asked, "How much do they cost?"

Jerome replied, "Obviously, they vary, but $50,000 is what I seem to have found out. For a kid from inner-city Chicago without any inheritance from my parents and financial aid still to pay back, I don't have the money."

Keaven grabbed his checkbook, looked, and saw, after satisfying all his debts of 9/11, that he had $51,000 left.

Keaven continued, "You know a good doctor who has done the surgery many times successfully before?"

Jerome said, "Yes."

Keaven went on, "You're committed to this surgery and really believe it will help you overcome the obstacles put in your way by employers and girls?"

Jerome replied, "Yes."

"Make an appointment for the surgery," Keaven commanded.

"What do you mean? I don't have the money," Jerome countered.

"I know. I do," Keaven responded.

"You don't even know me," Jerome replied. "I could use it for drugs like my parents."

"Look. I trust you with the money, but I'll pay the doctor myself.

Thus, there are no worries about the money not being used for the intended purpose," Keaven continued.

"Why would you do that for me?" Jerome asked. "We don't look alike, we're from different places, and you really don't know anything about me?"

"I know all that I need to know. Your life would be improved with the surgery, and I have the money for it," Keaven finished.

"I won't be able to pay you back any time soon," Jerome replied.

"Don't worry about it," Keaven commented.

Jerome said with distrust, "I mean. What do you want from me for doing this for me?"

Keaven replied, "Nothing. Just pursue your dreams soon without any obstacles."

Jerome continued, "I'm not much into hugging, but can I hug you, Big Brother?"

Keaven responded, "Sure." The two hugged then.

"I will repay you someday," Jerome assured him.

"Don't worry about it. Knowing that I could help you out is reward enough," Keaven finished.

19 NEWEST CIA FIELD AGENT

Keaven followed Matt's advice to the letter, graduating in spring 2003. He completed his studies top of his class in two years, emphasizing tax. Keaven even worked on his Arabic to ensure he would be ready for the challenge. Best of all then, he had found a job at the world's largest firm, the only one in fact with offices in every Middle Eastern and Southeastern Asian country. A better cover the CIA could not have provided itself.

Matt was impressed and ready to let Keaven begin. However, Keaven had a request. Keaven said, "You only get me if you hire Jerome, too."

Matt replied, "I thought we had a deal. Besides, who is this Jerome?"

Keaven said, "I'm kind of like his big brother. He had a hearing impairment that I helped him correct with cochlear implant surgery. He has a job now, but it is beneath his abilities. I want him on the team. His loyalty to me is absolute. I need someone I can trust besides just you."

Matt relented, "We're doing this off the books as it is. I'll hire him as an intelligence analyst related to this specific charge of catching the man responsible for 9/11." Matt continued, "Of course, we all know Osama bin Laden's the name. Catching him is still the game."

"Any luck catching the mole?" Keaven asked.

"No, which is why this mission is still off the books," Matt responded. "I almost believe our lack of significant progress in catching bin Laden has been the result of the mole feeding information to him to keep him from our grasp. That's just paranoia probably, but it could be the case as well."

"Because of my skill with Arabic, I asked for a rotation in the firm in Islamabad, Pakistan," Keaven continued. "The firm's sending me there first because of the great demand for a tax professional but especially for an attorney who can speak Arabic and English. As you know already, I can balance my time between work at the firm and the real job of catching bin Laden."

Matt replied, "We're on a secure phone line, so I can say this fact. While many still believe he's hidden in Afghanistan, I believe he's in Pakistan. The question is where. The other question is how to find out where. He's a national hero there. Nobody's planning just to hand him over to us, least of whom the Pakistani government for fear of risking civil war."

Keaven responded, "All right."

Matt finished, "Your bank account from the CIA to help fund your investigations and hiring of operatives is in the mail. You'll receive it as part of a bogus mailing to your office in Islamabad, saying you just won the Publisher's Clearinghouse Sweepstakes. The number in that filing is the bank account."

Keaven replied, "How creative."

All roads to bin Laden seemed to be through Benazir Bhutto, the first female leader of a Muslim country, Pakistan. As she led Pakistan from 1988 through the 1990s either as Prime Minister or the opposition leader, her primary goal was to make Pakistan a nuclear power. India, Pakistan's bitter foe, had nuclear weapons, so she believed such pursuit to be a necessity for detente. As India proposed nuclear weapons tests, she became further entrenched in this goal.

Concerned with Pakistan's nuclear weapons ambitions, the US government passed the Pressler Amendment. It imposed US financial and military embargoes to discourage continued pursuit of a nuclear weapons program. These embargoes significantly damaged Pakistan's economy and therein Bhutto's hold on power. Bhutto constantly pleaded for repeal, but her appeals fell on deaf ears.

Seeking revenge, Bhutto made many state visits to Libya, becoming close friends with Muammar al-Gaddafi. Further enraging the US government, Benazir Bhutto not only continued the Pakistani nuclear weapons program but also personally conveyed nuclear weapons technology to North Korea in exchange for missile technology in 1990 and 1996.

Worst then of all, she began responding to every Indian proposed nuclear weapons test with her own proposed Pakistani test. Nuclear proliferation in Southeast Asia became a big problem. Japan encouraged the US to act. However, Executive Order 12333 was firmly in place, not permitting assassinations of other countries' leaders.

In the late 1990s, she helped the Taliban gain control of Afghanistan, setting into motion the events leading to 9/11. After all, Bhutto had sent Pakistani forces to fight with the Taliban against the communist government remnants and then provided financial aid to support Taliban rule. As she already had provided nuclear weapons technology to North Korea, a country with whom Pakistan had no ongoing relationship, how much more likely was Bhutto to provide such technology to the Taliban, with whom Pakistan had an ongoing relationship? It became a huge issue for both the US government and the CIA.

With Executive Order 12333 firmly in place, the CIA could do little or nothing except: Suddenly, Swiss bank accounts with her family's name on them appeared. Apparently they appeared out of nowhere. Her husband was imprisoned on corruption charges, and she fled the country to Dubai.

Thus, Keaven would have a stop-over in his flight to Islamabad, namely Dubai, United Arab Emirates. There, he would seek to meet with Benazir thanks to some diplomatic help from Matt. He was introduced as an international tax attorney who could help with her corruption charges related to setting up shell companies to funnel kickbacks and Iraq oil-for-food program money to herself. In the end then, all corporate matters ultimately revolved around tax treatment.

Bhutto had studied at Radcliffe College of Harvard University and then at Oxford University. She knew English, so Keaven did not have to face an early test of his Arabic.

Keaven began in private with her, "I'm not going to waste our time here. We both know that your corruption charges are the direct result of the CIA framing you to get you out of office. I may or may not be able to help you in this regard. How much I help you directly relates to how many contacts you still have with the Taliban and Pakistan's intelligence community and how much good information you provide to me."

Benazir responded, "You're pretty confident for somebody so new at this game."

Keaven replied, "Yes, I've just begun my legal career overseas."

"You know that's not what I meant," Benazir countered.

"Just because I know the CIA's responsible for your current exile doesn't mean that I work for the CIA. It just means that I'm a good attorney, finding the right answer to the right question," Keaven responded.

"If you want to play it that way, then fine," Benazir continued.

"So how are your connections with the Taliban and Pakistani intelligence?" Keaven continued.

"I know whom you want," Benazir continued.

"Which of course doesn't answer either of my questions," Keaven continued.

"Even if I knew, I'm not giving him to you," Benazir responded.

Keaven turned to an aggressive approach, grabbing her by the shoulder, saying, "3,000 dead. 6,000 injured. You think you and your family are safe?"

Benazir countered, "The US government did all it could to me. I'm in exile now because of it, away from my country. There's nothing more that the US government can do."

Keaven noticed her dictatorial reference to "MY country." "You're wrong," Keaven countered and then continued, "Let me tell you a little tale about Executive Orders. In 1976, Executive Order 11905 was issued in the wake of the Church Committee report on CIA assassination attempts on Fidel Castro, Ngo Dinh Diem, Patrice

Lumumba, Rene Schneider, and Rafael Trujillo. Executive Orders 12306 and 12333 continued the pre-emption that started in 1976: 'No person employed by or acting on behalf of the United States Government shall engage in, or conspire to engage in, assassination.' Following the events of 9/11, President Bush revoked these Executive Orders. He authorized what is current policy: 'targeted assassinations' of political leaders in 'rogue states' or who harbor 'international terrorism.' Do you understand, Benazir?"

Benazir countered, "I'm not the leader of Pakistan now."

Keaven replied, "You're still the leader of your political party whether it is in power or not and whether you are present in Pakistan or not."

"Are you threatening to kill me if I don't tell you where bin Laden?" Benazir countered.

"Obviously, I didn't say that . . . directly," Keaven continued.

Benazir mentioned, "You're acting like a terrorist."

Keaven responded, "One way or another, we will get bin Laden. The only question is whether you will help in that process or remain a footnote to history. By the way here, you're not untouchable. You have a family with you."

Benazir countered, "So you're threatening their lives now, too? What if I tell you I still do have Taliban and Pakistani intelligence contacts that I can use to kill you and your family?"

"I would say good," Keaven replied. "Those facts would mean you could help our mission."

Benazir continued, menace in her voice, "You're not scared?"

"Al-Qaeda, in one way or another, has already killed my parents, my father directly, my mother indirectly, removing her will to fight cancer, and my wife-to-be in 9/11." Keaven said. "As for me, I don't fear death. It will bring me closer to the ones who've been taken from me, so, unlike you, I am untouchable."

"If I get him for you, what do I get for it? Will your CIA, your government, allow me to return to my country from exile?" Benazir questioned.

"I can't speak for my government, but your cooperation would definitely be noticed," Keaven countered.

"I'll make some inquiries. Know that I will want the corruption charges to disappear in exchange for finding him," Benazir finished.

"I'll be in touch," Keaven acknowledged.

Years passed. Keaven relied on US intel from Matt and Pakistani intel from Benazir to search ten square miles of Pakistan each day, beginning with the most likely and ending with the least likely to contain bin Laden.

Computer in tow, he found a way to continue his cover job, legal work for companies in Pakistan and companies selling to Pakistan. His US-based firm had bought into cyber-commuting, allowing employees to work from home to save time from being wasted on commuting. Keaven could work on legal briefs and legal documents in the process of searching the country for bin Laden.

His career had progressed favorably, resulting in promotion to partner and a salary of more than $1 million each year. The money was meaningless, though, because it could not buy back his parents' lives or Tricia's life.

Keaven had ventured to possible sites in Afghanistan and Iran as well. Matt continually warned him that, if Keaven were caught, nobody would try to save him. He would just disappear. Obviously, Keaven could care less at this point. Many days, death seemed preferable to life. Bin Laden seemed to be a ghost. Keaven constantly wondered whether he had died many years ago with tapes faked to make him still seem alive.

He still had charity in mind as he traversed countries. Keaven brought deflated soccer balls with him on every Land Rover journey into the countryside. He had a pump with him. Any time he saw kids gathered around sock soccer balls or worse, Keaven would take out a ball and the pump, handing the kids the pumped-up ball. He consequently played so much with the kids that he became an excellent soccer player. The ball was meaningless in many ways in comparison to the food he brought to those without much or any at all.

One day, Keaven saved a child who was trapped under a wall. An earthquake had occurred that led to stones from the wall falling on the child. As usual, there were no newspapers or media around to record his heroism. There could not be. At the time, he remembered the owl he had seen long ago at Berkeley. More and more, it seemed like he was there to stand guard for others while they enjoyed their lives just like that owl served as a sentinel.

Soon it was 2007. Keaven had not found the great evil, the person responsible for killing Tricia. The whole situation was frustrating.

Pakistanis were obviously protecting bin Laden from being discovered. With Al-Qaeda's low-tech reliance on couriers, the NSA could be of little help.

Keaven finally acknowledged that only through Benazir's return to Pakistan could she renew the necessary contacts to find bin Laden. He negotiated through Matt, who somehow convinced the CIA to advocate to the President. Soon, US puppet, General Musharraf, under instructions from the US President, pardoned her, allowing her to return to Pakistan.

Finally returning in 2008, she instantly became the leading candidate for re-election as Pakistani leader. Instead of searching the countryside, Keaven now saw himself as her protector. So long as she was alive, the possibility of finding bin Laden was alive. He followed her from campaign stop to campaign stop. He almost had become her good luck charm. She began waving to him at campaign events. In a country that harbored so many terrorists, he was her security blanket.

For all that she had done, Keaven somehow felt like he was protecting his own mother. She was a special woman. At a campaign event one day, though, Keaven received a message on his cell phone from "God." Keaven had no clue what had happened to Mo up until that moment. Mo texted to him, "Get out of there." Despite the years of silence between the two of them, Keaven somehow knew he could trust God, so he followed orders like any good soldier would.

Keaven walked a distance to reach his Land Rover, eventually climbing in and wondering what was up. Before he communicated any more with God, Keaven looked in the distance to Benazir. She was looking plaintively right back at him. Keaven had seen that visage before in Tricia before she died, in Rosa before she was led back to her accuser, and in his mom as she acknowledged she would die from cancer. He took out the pictures from a special Christmas long ago: of Mo and Tricia and of Tricia and Keaven.

"What's up, God?" Keaven texted back.

Mo emailed, "I've worked at the NSA ever since the day Tricia was killed. I have spyware on all your tech. I've been watching out for you since that day whether it was at Illinois or in the outback of Pakistan. I've hacked drone cameras and anything else that would help me watch over you. Thankfully enough, I've been able to intervene where necessary through the years without even gaining your attention. Unfortunately, you need my direct intervention now. Call me at this phone number."

Keaven dialed the number. He was then talking to Mo for the first time in years. "Why did I have to get out of there?"

Mo said, "She's going to be assassinated."

Keaven stopped the car on its way out of town and circled back. Mo said, "Stop."

"How do you know what I'm doing?" Keaven questioned.

"There's more than one drone in the area, watching her," Mo countered. "I can see you in the drones' video."

"I have to protect her," Keaven protested.

Mo said, "The time for protecting her is over. A Pakistani intel officer is willing to give us bin Laden's location for $25 million and for letting Benazir get assassinated."

"You really believe that he knows where bin Laden is?" Keaven questioned.

Mo continued, "They've known since at least 2006. They've been using him as a bargaining chip to deal with militant groups in their own country and in Afghanistan."

"So in other words, I've just been wasting my time," Keaven intoned.

Mo answered, "Yes."

"Despite enabling the Taliban, who then enabled 9/11, and transferring nuclear technology to North Korea, Benazir doesn't deserve to die," Keaven remarked.

"Don't tell me you fell for her, too," Mo countered. "She's the devil in disguise just as much as Chel was."

"Still," Keaven continued, wanting to do something to stop whatever was to befall her. Suddenly, he heard the deafening boom of high explosives. Keaven did not look back. He also did not want to know whether the US had killed her in a drone strike or whether Pakistani intel or radicals had actually detonated the explosives. Some things, he just did not want to know.

Mo continued, "I thought you learned enough from falling for Chel that evil was evil, unchangeable, but you seem to have a soft-spot for evil women." Mo was in full rage mode.

Keaven replied, "You'll never forgive me. Will you?"

"Tricia knew you were in Boston. She didn't want to be a stalker, so she found a job in the nearest big city to be close enough to you, hoping to reconnect with you someday," Mo continued. "You weren't worth it."

"Thanks, Mo," Keaven remarked. "Great words from a former friend." Keaven continued, "I tried to save her."

"I've watched over you all these years because I believed in your mission, not necessarily in you," Mo countered.

Keaven sarcastically countered, "Thank you."

Mo replied, "You've tried my patience over the years."

Keaven answered, "Now you don't need me. Right? You've found bin Laden."

"I've watched over you so long that it will be difficult for me to stop," Mo continued. "Who knows? You could still redeem yourself by becoming President."

"Before you find out officially, I bet I can tell you where bin Laden is," Keaven remarked.

"If you knew, that I would already know. I don't know, so . . . ?" Mo countered.

"He's in the compound, Bilal Town, Abbottabad, Pakistan," Keaven remarked.

Mo questioned, "What are you talking about?"

"This morning, Benazir tipped me off to a strange compound built there, located near the Pakistan-Afghanistan border," Keaven remarked. "She had shared information with me so many times before, but, this time, she glowed on sharing it. It was as if she knew she had finally discovered the key to help me."

Mo continued, "Meaning what?"

Keaven remarked, "Now that she's been killed, it's obvious that she asked the right person the right question at the right time and finally had the right answer but was killed for discovering that information."

Mo remarked, "You're right."

"How do you know?" Keaven countered.

Mo gravely continued, "Seeing conclusive proof of Benazir's death, the intel officer just revealed the location to his CIA contact. It's exactly what you mentioned."

"Somehow, I feel like I didn't do enough yet again to save a life," Keaven plaintively replied. "Especially now, she did not have to die."

"The CIA director has decided not to inform the President under the theory that the organization cannot afford to be wrong again," Mo responded.

Keaven countered, "Why do you hack?"

"I'm legit because I follow NSA rules. You finally can be proud of me," Mo replied.

Keaven answered, "I've always been proud of you like Tricia was."

"I've had to deal with this anger for years, blaming you for Tricia's death," Mo continued. "You've been too good of a friend, really my only friend, for my hate to last. I finally forgive you."

"I guess all I can say is thank you, not only for the forgiveness but for watching over me all these years," Keaven replied.

Part of the reason for the CIA leader's inaction was anger over how the Bush administration had ordered the intelligence organization to manipulate intel data to convince the world of the Iraq's imminent threat with weapons of mass destruction. The proud CIA also had much of their powers stripped after 9/11 for somehow being responsible for not stopping Al Qaeda. These two salvoes from the Bush administration were enough for the CIA to maintain the confidentiality of this information for the next President to use and benefit from in public sentiment. Just to ensure this theory did not ever gain traction in the non-intel community, the CIA waited some years into the new President's term of office before revealing the intel.

In the meantime then, a CIA unit was stationed to monitor movements at the compound over those years to ensure the wolf did not escape the noose. However, Keaven had to stand sentinel to ensure that the unit truly accomplished its objective. Thus, Mo was watching over Keaven as Keaven watched over the CIA unit. The agents in that unit in turn watched over bin Laden.

Finally, it was the proper time for the new President to get credit for taking down bin Laden. Operation Neptune Spear, involving a SEAL team and a helicopter insertion, would result in the killing or capturing of bin Laden at the compound.

Matt told Keaven the details, ordering him to stay out of it. The plan was about to commence on May 1. To ensure no unnecessary interventions, the CIA observation team had been ordered out of country days before. Drones took their place in terms of standing guard.

Keaven was the lone human observer left. He was working on

documents to incorporate a new Coca-Cola bottler in Pakistan, all the while anticipating the coming secret forces intervention. Suddenly, he heard helicopters in the distance. Keaven checked the time on his cell phone. It was too early. Matt told him the SEAL team would not be present until a couple of hours from now. Was Matt lying to him about the real operation time, losing faith in Keaven's ability to maintain confidential information?

Keaven stopped work on his cover job and took out night-vision binoculars. He quickly identified the approaching helicopters as Russian Kazan Ansat's. The Russian intelligence community utilized them. This version typically had a pilot and ten passengers as maximum capacity in each. Keaven noticed two helicopters on approach to the compound. His mind turned to why the Russians would be here, especially now.

Mo evidently was paying attention. He texted, "Look up."

Keaven emailed back, "I'm on it."

Mo texted, "Mole in CIA sent word of mission to Russian intelligence."

Keaven replied, "What do they want?"

Mo responded, "Even God doesn't know but can guess."

The two helicopters landed close to Keaven. Ten armed Russian intelligence officers departed the helicopters. Soon, Keaven heard a familiar voice and instantly identified it. Keaven knew it was Vlad Putrin, his archenemy from UNIS.

Whether it would help or not, Keaven messaged Mo: "Ten Russian intelligence agents, including Vlad Putrin, approaching compound."

Mo countered, "Vlad Putrin?"

Keaven replied, "Yes."

Mo answered, "He's in the database as a CIA agent."

Keaven, surprised, remarked, "Well, we've discovered the mole then." Keaven stopped conversing with Mo, attention fully turned to the compound.

The agents walked into the compound and were leading out a tall figure, most likely bin Laden himself. Bin Laden was not in restraints. It looked in fact like Vlad was in the midst of a conversation with an old friend. Al Qaeda and the Russians had fought during the Afghanistan wars, so how could they ever be friends? It was obvious that Vlad's evil intent was to foil the American plan to kill or capture bin Laden. Soon, the Russian agents would be airlifting bin Laden to a safe location who knows where. The US would never capture him then, and Keaven's promise to Tricia would never come to fruition.

Keaven did not carry a weapon with him. He was an off-the-books CIA agent to begin. Carrying a gun would be dangerous. Its discovery would have blown his cover. His only weapons then were ten deflated soccer balls, a pump, snacks, a backpack, a computer, a cell phone, night-vision binoculars, and the Land Rover.

The Russians, though, had made a crucial error. They parked their two helicopters too close together. Keaven grabbed a heavy stone, climbed into the Land Rover, put the stone on the accelerator, and turned the ignition key while standing outside the vehicle. Suddenly, the Land Rover lurched forward, gradually accelerating to top pace. It took out the nearer helicopter at its fuel tank, causing an explosion that destroyed the second helicopter as well.

Now it was just Keaven versus ten Russian agents and bin Laden. The explosion certainly caught the attention of the drone operators. The CIA would know something was up now. Vlad knew this fact as well. He was wearing a black ski mask covering most of his face except for the wide slit from his left eye to his right eye. Obviously Keaven knew him by his voice. Suddenly, Vlad, despite the facial covering, sent the nine remaining members of his Russian agents off into the distance to find their own ways out of the area. Vlad then walked bin Laden back to the house.

Foiling the US plan had been Vlad's obvious intent. However, once the explosion occurred, tipping the CIA off to his presence, Vlad's attention turned to maintaining his own secret cover. The first step was returning bin Laden to his compound, and the second step was running away from the area.

With the Russian agents gone for more than ten minutes, Keaven began to notice activity in the compound, a vehicle being loaded. Then four men appeared. Bin Laden could be making a get-away attempt.

Based on watching the compound for so long, Keaven knew well that the four figures were bin Laden, his son, his primary courier, and the courier's brother. They had AK-47s and handguns. Keaven obviously had no weapons to begin, now had no vehicle, and, thus, seemed to have little or no chance at stopping them. For a moment, his promise to Tricia seemed impossible to fulfill. Thankfully, a CIA drone fired a missile, destroying the vehicle before the four could get in it and get away.

Their plan turned to running away. In an assault similar to his self-defense actions against the 11th Street gang in San Francisco so many years ago, Keaven dispatched of the four men, rendering them unconscious. He carried them back inside the compound.

Timing was everything then. After completing this job, Keaven heard US helicopters in the distance. While they were stealth helicopters, he knew what to listen for and could hear them coming.

The four men of evil would not be unconscious for long. Keaven had personally knocked out bin Laden last and spent a moment taking in this visage of evil, another indelible image for his memories.

It was the man responsible for killing Tricia. Keaven wanted to kill him, but he knew that bringing him to justice, not death, had been his personal objective. For a moment, he could take pride in stopping Vlad from helping bin Laden escape and then in stopping the four himself in yet another escape attempt. Somehow, though, Keaven knew that he would have to confront Vlad again in the future. For now, though, all the years he had spent in Pakistan finally seemed to have been worthwhile.

As the accounts of the action were written, Keaven was fine with being omitted. Only Matt, Mo, and anybody viewing the drone videos would know he had been there. Keaven was a little surprised that the team had ultimately killed bin Laden. That evil individual could have awakened, run inside the compound, and hidden as a last attempt to survive the oncoming SEALs. However, Keaven still had hoped that he would have been brought to justice, not to death, in the process. The safety of the SEALs, though, had to be paramount of course.

Keaven put on his backpack and began walking and hitchhiking his way back to Islamabad. Tomorrow would be the last day at his job, the real one and the cover one. He had made a promise in Tricia's memory and had fulfilled it. Now all that was left was to find a way to get to Heaven, or so Keaven thought.

Matt had asked Keaven for permission to honor his service. Keaven knew from the moment he had taken the job off the books that he could never receive recognition for what he had done for his country. The CIA was off the books as it was, let alone somebody off the books from the CIA itself.

Almost out of distance from the compound, Keaven stopped a second to look back. He took out the picture of Mo and Tricia and then of Tricia and himself. There was not much light, but Keaven could make out the contours of the compound and of the faces in the pictures. He said, "Rest in peace, Tricia." Then Keaven said, "Thank you, God, for watching over me this whole journey, protecting me so that I could fulfill my promise to Tricia."

20 WHAT NOW?

Matt had informed Keaven that Vlad never returned to the CIA, or else they would have charged him with treason. Matt guessed that Vlad would join the Russian intelligence community. Keaven believed Vlad would quickly rise to the President of Russia, his rendezvous with destiny.

Keaven thanked Matt for allowing him to play a role in the mission albeit off the books. Matt tried to encourage him to become part of the US intelligence community on the books. He cajoled that, with the mole likely out of the picture, it could be a rewarding and safe career. Keaven declined.

Mo had communicated more with Keaven, trying to encourage him to run for President against the then-current Democrat in the White House. Sitting in May 2011, Keaven knew he was already too late to try to enter the Republican field for the 2012 nomination and election. Besides, Keaven was still registered as an Independent.

Remembering his vow in Rosa's memory, Keaven turned to charitable work. He had more than enough money from his cover career. He had no interest in buying fancy cars or time with fancy women. He started a Christmas tradition of dressing up as Santa and distributing gifts he had purchased to children in hospitals. After all, he did not have any kids of his own, meaning that every kid could be his indirectly just as every person in America was indirectly part of his family.

With his legal and tax knowledge, he helped not-for-profits incorporate and apply for 501(c)(3) tax-exempt status. Keaven also helped on tax returns for the poor as part of the IRS's Volunteer Income Tax Assistance program. He also volunteered for legal aid societies, providing pro bono representation for indigent clients. Given his significant donations to charities of time and money, Keaven was soon serving as a director on many boards, including the Points of Light Board and the Ronald Reagan Presidential Foundation Board of Trustees.

However, all these efforts could not cover up the past. While Keaven had been devoted to catching bin Laden, he never had to deal with Tricia's death. With the objective satisfied, though, he started suffering from re-play after re-play of Tricia's death moving through his mind hour after hour day after day. It was getting to the point where he was having difficulty dealing with it.

He started to work with all-night basketball leagues in urban areas so that he would not have to experience any bad dreams. The programs were designed to stop gangs from recruiting new initiates and from engaging in illegal activities, so again he was helping the community out in the course of trying to save himself. Obviously, his experience with the 11th Street gang in San Francisco had a part to play in this choice. The amount of time he spent volunteering started to alarm his fellow volunteers. They started questioning whether he needed help himself.

Then something else captured his attention. Keaven had known the Affordable Care Act (ACA) had been passed in 2010. However, he had not been in country. It did not really capture his full notice until the Supreme Court ruled on its constitutionality in 2012.

A tax attorney by former trade and a Constitutional scholar from long ago, he became incensed. The Supreme Court had acknowledged the ACA as unconstitutional under the Commerce Clause, the tool that liberal justices used to extend the power of government beyond the framers' words.

However, the Court ended up finding the ACA constitutional. The grounds were that the penalty imposed on those citizens who did not obtain health insurance coverage was a tax. As a tax, Congress had the constitutional power to pass such legislation.

Keaven knew taxes and the Constitution like no other. The Supreme Court had risen to become a legislative branch in this decision if it had not already done so long before. The problem was that, with lifetime appointments, they did not face the accountability of elections like real legislators.

While Tricia would remain in his mind forever, Keaven had found a new cause, a reason for living until it was time to reunite with Tricia, Rosa, and his parents now in Heaven.

To gain the credentials to be able to criticize the decision and other unconstitutional or at least unfair provisions in the Internal Revenue Code itself, Keaven decided to become a professor. With his successful legal career and studies, he soon found placement at a public university. It gave him the opportunity to critique all that was wrong with the Internal Revenue Code but especially with the ACA Supreme Court decision. While he had to quit some boards, Keaven remained on the Points of Light and Ronald Reagan Presidential Foundation boards.

Mo again tried to cajole Keaven into entering another Presidential race, the 2016 election cycle as a candidate for the Republican nomination. An inner sense told him not to get involved. There was something about the candidate Neville Truism that at least initially inspired confidence that change would come. Unfortunately, too late for Keaven to enter the field, he learned that Truism was anything but a truism.

In fact, Truism seemed to end up representing every "ism" known to humankind: sexism, racism, isolationism, nationalism, liberalism, even in some respects socialism, surprisingly Communism for his growing respect for Russia and its façade of capitalism, and finally egotism. Unfortunately, conservatism seemed to be the one "ism" that Truism did not countenance.

Keaven knew he did not have the name recognition of Truism and probably would have stood no chance against him. However, he forever regretted not finding a way for the citizens of the country to have a choice in the 2016 election other than the lesser of two evils. Keaven, still an Independent, could rightly critique both candidates but was unable to change the events that would soon unfold.

Keaven hoped and prayed for the best. At first, Truism did his best (or worst, totally reliant on a person's perspective), driving out undocumented aliens, building a wall, overturning parts of the ACA, cutting taxes on the rich, reducing foreign aid, disavowing treaty obligations under NATO and other provisions, turning the world's protection over to Russia and China, and installing an Independent justice to the Supreme Court. Simultaneously, he did nothing to check the growth of recreational drug use, to help the indigent, or to end divisiveness. In fact, he seemed to be doing everything possible to drive Americans farther apart. Instead of making American great, he had made America hate.

Truism executed all these moves without hesitation. Overturning parts of the ACA was the right move for all Americans because the program had resulted in higher costs for health care than before its creation. Cutting taxes stimulated the economy. Reducing foreign aid helped lead to balanced budgets. Installing an Independent justice to the Supreme Court made it seem to be more balanced and representative of the population with four Republicans, four Democrats, and an Independent. However, the Independent nominee before confirmation soon became a Democratic justice after confirmation just as David Souter had under the first President Bush.

Disavowing treaty obligations, though, was problematic. Soon enough, Russia, now a friend again, recaptured the Baltic states in a Blitzkrieg reminiscent of the Nazis during World War II. Nary a shot had to be fired. Without the US participating in a NATO-backed response, other nations quickly retreated from their mutual defense obligations. Nobody wanted war in the end, so Russia had nothing in its way.

As Keaven had expected, Vlad Putrin quickly rose through the ranks of Russian leadership. He had become the default leader of a faux capitalist country. Russia was capitalist in name only and actually had returned to many aspects of Communism.

Meanwhile, China invaded Taiwan, reclaimed it, and started

provoking Japan. Concern over war led to stock market crashes worldwide. The world began to enter a Great Depression. How were the markets and consumers supposed to react in the face of possible world wars? The prospects certainly reduced consumer sentiment.

Divisiveness in the country reached record proportions. Everybody wanted to believe the divisiveness would dial down following the election. Instead, Truism did everything he could to ramp it up. Hate crimes rose exponentially year after year.

Keaven finally had enough. He set up a political action committee to begin funding a run for President of the US, beginning with the Republican primaries. Obviously, the heaviest burden was finally shifting his Independent voter registration to Republican. He took pride in his ability to critique both parties as an Independent. However, at the end of the day, Keaven knew who he was. He always was a Republican in everything but name.

Challenging Truism in the 2020 Republican primary seemed futile. Sitting Presidents do not get replaced in their party's primaries as they faced the best prospects of maintaining a party's control of the White House. Sometimes, a voice in opposition, though, was necessary to remind the sitting President of his base. If all Keaven would ever be is a voice in the darkness, then he was ready to serve that role.

Keaven's first tax professorship had been at the University of New Hampshire from 2011 to 2017. New Hampshire had learned of his great commitment to volunteerism and the state's political interests.

In 2017, he accepted a job as a tax professor at the University of

Northern Iowa. He knew what he was doing, and soon Iowa would know what he was about, too. He would be working in the state where the next Republican nominees for President of the US would be chosen. While the presumptive nominee Truism would not likely campaign there much, Keaven would.

Eventually he quit his teaching job and formally announced his campaign for the Republican nomination for President against Truism. God was his campaign manager, and Mo could fill the role like no other. He did not pursue the office for personal gratification.

As he announced, Keaven said the following: "I am Keaven Deal, who grew up in a household of a special forces soldier and a special mother who gave me a love of learning, including the Bible and the Constitution. I am here today because it is high time that somebody tells Neville Truism that he's done.

Yes, Neville Truism, a reality television star, deserves an Academy Award for how well he pulled the wool over all our eyes. In fact, his comb-over is the all-too-appropriate metaphor.

He professed to be a Republican. He wanted to be known as the next Ronald Reagan. Unfortunately, Ronald Reagan is rolling over in his grave right now. Checking the Soviets, now the Russians, was Reagan's primary objective of foreign policy. Ending recreational drug use was a notable objective of Reagan's domestic policy as was the desire to have every person treated equally based on the content of their character, not the color of their skin. All these Reagan values have never been more in danger.

No, the only Republican Neville Truism will seemingly ever be akin to is Herbert Hoover. Just as Hoover did, Truism is presiding over the dissolution of the best economy in the world, another Great Depression at our doorstep.

Meanwhile, the world is at a tipping point, set for war, unless the US is willing to reclaim its position simply of guaranteeing treaty obligations. Standing together with the rest of the world is enough to check Russia's and China's ambitions. Guaranteeing treaties does not encourage war but instead averts it.

We should have known better. Truism long ago remarked on the King show that Democrats made the best Presidents with regard to the economy. King quickly pointed out the flaw in his reasoning, mentioning President Carter was a Democrat and presided over one of the worst economies in the history of America.

Let me help you out with something, Truism. Republican has these parts, 're,' 'public,' and 'can.' The job of a true Republican is to let the 'public' do what they 'can' 're' as in again. It simply means that we are the party that permits the public to do what it can on its own again free from governmental interference.

Our citizens know better how to provide for need in their own communities than the government in DC. They unfortunately have to pay so much in taxes that they do not have enough left over to help their own. Meanwhile, you, Truism, continue to allow government to grow bigger, allowing it to act as if it knows better than American citizens how best to spend their own money. You're creating a debt that future generations will be paying off for years to come.

As for my goal, I intend to be the next Abraham Lincoln and Ronald Reagan. Right now, these two Republican Presidents would not even be welcomed into our party. That fact should shame our base, illustrating the error in our ways.

In challenging times like these in particular, I find solace in Dr. Joseph Warren's 'Boston Massacre Oration.' It provides us with the guiding light in a time of darkness, 'Our country is in danger but not to be despaired of . . . . Our enemies are numerous and powerful, but . . . Heaven and earth will aid the resolution. On you [rely] the fortunes of America. You are to decide the important questions on which rest the happiness and the liberty of millions yet unborn. Act worthy of yourselves.'

I intend to do so. Because Truism is incapable of doing so, that's why I stand here today. God, forever bless America. Thank you."

After his strong announcement, a reporter asked Keaven, "What do you in particular have to offer? You can't beat Truism."

Keaven responded, "You'll learn what I have to offer in coming days. As for who wins the primaries, that's not up to the press. It's up to all the Republican citizens of this country and, ultimately, all the citizens of this country."

The reporter shouted as Keaven walked away, "At least tell us about why you are wearing so many rubber bracelets." Even though he had been wearing a suit, all the reporters could notice that he had rubber bracelets on his writs.

Keaven relented, "All right," and continued, "On my right wrist, I wear two rubber bracelets: 'WWRD' (W.W.R.D.) and 'WWGD'

(W.W.G.D.). On my left wrist, I wear two rubber bracelets: 'WWLD' (W.W.L.D.) and the name of a soldier who perished in serving in our country's military."

The reporter continued, "What do they stand for?"

Keaven replied, "WWRD stands for 'What would Reagan do?' WWGD stands for 'What would God, George Washington, Old Glory, or God, my campaign manager Mo, do?' I'll let you guess which of those G's it really represents. WWLD stands for 'What would Lincoln do?' Finally, the name of the soldier who perished in serving in our country's military that is on my wrist today is Darren Deal, my father. These four bracelets guide the decisions I make. Not surprisingly, they all provide the same guidance and same answers, never disagreeing."

The reporter became quiet. Keaven saw a look of admiration on his face.

Soon Keaven received a call from the Republican National Committee (RNC) chairman, asking him not to challenge Truism in the primary. He began, "Truism has the best chance of re-election. All the other potential Republican candidates are smart enough to step to the side, unifying together."

Keaven responded, "No, they're not stepping aside because they want to unify. They're not running because they know they cannot beat him."

The RNC chairman retorted, "They'd stand a better chance of beating him than you. I'm sorry to say that you're a nobody."

"Everybody is a nobody until they become a somebody, and I

intend to become a somebody," Keaven countered.

"Even if you would beat him, it could cost us the White House," the RNC chairman replied. "Truism would run as an Independent, and all you would do is cost him Republican supporters in the process. You'd hand the White House to the Democrats. Is that what you want then?"

"Truism must be made accountable to his base," Keaven continued. "Otherwise, in the next election, the only choice will be between a Democrat who calls himself a Republican and a Democrat. In reality, the Democrats will be assured of the White House if I don't provide a credible alternative."

"Stay out of it, and I assure you my support during the next election cycle," the RNC chairman replied.

"You don't seem to understand that there may never be another election at the rate this world is falling apart," Keaven implored. "Also, you tell all the candidates the same thing: "Stay out of the race, and I'll support you during the next cycle." Right?"

The RNC chairman continued, "What do you want? I obviously know donors. Do you want a high-paying job? Do you want a post in Truism's government? What can I offer you to stay out of it?"

Keaven replied, "My soul is not for sale. I have more money than I'll ever require, and I don't want anything but for my country to be restored to its greatness."

The RNC chairman replied, "Well, to minimize the damage then, to show you how futile the effort will be, I'll allow only one Republican debate."

"Is that decision really yours alone?" Keaven asked.

"It's the mutual desire of Truism's campaign and mine," the RNC leader replied.

"So much for freedom of speech and debate," Keaven ventured.

"Just remember that I warned you that you would accomplish nothing and stand no chance," the RNC chairman countered.

21 THE DEBATE

The debate moderator was a woman. She began, "First, you candidates will make your opening statements."

Truism began: "This debate is a waste of time. I have more important matters in this country and world to deal with. However, all you need to know is that my opponent was an Independent so recently and all of a sudden thinks he's a Republican. I've been a Republican for much longer.

As to accomplishments, what has this loser done? I've been one of the greatest businessmen in the history of the world. I have built empires. I have a family. This loser is single. He probably has never been on a date.

As President, I repealed parts of the ACA, enacted a tax cut, appointed a Supreme Court justice, and oversaw so many positives for the US. This loser has never been in office. What more needs to be said. I'm the winner. He's the loser.

Would you ever vote for a loser, who would lose the White House to whomever the Democratic nominee is? Again, I have better things to do with my time than debate a nobody."

The moderator then told, Keaven, "It's your turn, but please try to refrain from inflammatory characterizations or accusations."

Keaven replied, "Do you mean I cannot tell the world what it already knows? Neville Truism is sexist and racist; only believes in women as a pursuit, not as an equal; wants America to be completely white; is a sexual predator; is the biggest liar in the history of American politics; and sadly is the farthest thing away from being a

Republican that this party has ever seen?"

The moderator responded with a sigh, "Yes, I mean exactly that type of language."

"Okay. Then I'll refrain from using any of that language," Keaven replied.

The audience laughed for a moment.

Truism intervened, saying, "I deserve a right to respond."

"It's my turn," Keaven remarked.

Truism retorted, "You've already had your opening remarks."

"I was asking a question, and now I'll be making my opening remarks," Keaven continued.

Truism continued, "You're a loser."

"Takes one to know one," Keaven replied.

Keaven then began his opening remarks, "This party is the party of Lincoln and Reagan. We cite each name many times but do not even remember what they taught us. They believed individuals should be judged based on the content of their characters, not the color of their skins. Lincoln died because of this belief and the belief in one America. Reagan constantly spoke of equality. Where one American suffers, we all suffer. They both made faith paramount in their lives. Where is faith today?

Neville Truism certainly has evidenced he does not need faith to guide his decisions. Goldfish are given more rights and protections than human embryos and fetuses.

He believes government knows better how to spend your money than you do. He has not fundamentally changed the tax system to be fair. Why is it that the wealthy are given all these itemized deductions for mortgage insurance and mortgage interest while those who can afford only rent are denied any deductions for this expense? Why is it that corporations are allowed to get away with tax fraud, but individuals are tried, convicted, and jailed of it on a daily basis?

Government is meant to work side by side, being fair in the process. Government is not meant to be masters to citizens or to pick winners and losers. The idea of freedom from governmental interference is at the core of Republicanism. 'Re,' 'public,' and 'can' stand for something: The public can, again, do for themselves. Americans don't require the government to do for them what they can already do for themselves more effectively and efficiently.

No more evidence is necessary of Neville Truism's commitment to re-election over the simple demands of the Republican party base. He said 'until Death do us part' six times, but he parted before death six times. He said he was a Democrat until he became a Republican just to win an election.

He went bankrupt twelve times. One bankruptcy is sufficient in of itself to be barred from ever serving as a director of a publicly traded company. If he could not serve on the board of any company, how is it that we have allowed him to serve on the board of the most sacred of companies, the US economy?

At the same time, he tells us that the poor will always be poor, so why help them? Truism is a living embodiment of the government saving him from poverty, having debt on debt cancelled through these bankruptcies by the grace of the government.

He's been wealthy his whole life and now been present in DC for the last few years. He does not know what it is to be an ordinary American struggling, so how can he possibly help an ordinary American who is struggling? He certainly has not created any more jobs during his administration, and the economy is at historical lows.

Neville Truism, it's high time somebody told you that you're done."

The debate progressed with increasing animosity.

During his closing remarks, Keaven said, "How could we have expected somebody who has so little time for the Ten Commandments to have any time for defending the Bill of Rights? He allegedly has committed 'high crimes and misdemeanors' and therein could be impeached his next term.

If he is not defeated or impeached, please heed my warning: Without the threat of re-election facing him during his second term, he will become not only the most liberal Republican President ever but also the most liberal President ever."

Truism walked across the stage and punched Keaven in the mouth. Keaven went down like a sack of potatoes because of the sucker punch. Keaven was soon conscious again, rose to his feet, and wiped the blood from his mouth.

The moderator commented, "Are you sure you want to continue?"

Keaven replied, "Yes."

She then said, looking at his bloodied and bruised face, "You look like hell."

"You're not the first woman to tell me that," Keaven remarked.

The audience laughed and applauded him for returning to his feet.

Keaven continued, "At least now, everybody knows why I'm still single. Of course, it doesn't help when individuals like Neville Truism are with multiple women at the same time. It just makes it more difficult for a regular guy to find a great gal."

Truism started to make his way back over the stage to hit Keaven again. The Secret Service rushed on the stage to restrain him this time.

Keaven commented, "I have no problem turning my cheek for you to hit me again, but I prefer to believe in the rule: Fool me once; shame on you; fool me twice; shame on me.

The problem for you is the American people believe in the same rule. Many Republicans now understand who you really are so that you will not fool them again with your Republicanism in name only and liberalism in reality.

By the way, Neville, you're also helping me teach kids tonight about bullies. The only way to stop a bully is to stand up to them.

How do you like that, Neville? Somebody is finally standing up to your bullying. Who's the loser now?"

Republican voters then voted in their primaries. As everybody had expected, Neville went on to win. However, at least Keaven had put his feet to the fire, making him acknowledge that he was a Republican nominee. As Truism returned to the White House, easily dispatching of his Democratic opponent, Keaven's warning became all too prophetic. Truism turned left like no other before.

The moment Keaven lost the primaries, he had a new endeavor. Somebody had to stand guard while others enjoyed their lives. Cuba was the new destination based on some nefarious Russian interventions. Keaven would find some way to help. Whether he was biding his time for the next election or not did not matter at that point.

22 CUBA NOW

Keaven asked Matt for an insertion into Cuba to be able to play a role in monitoring developments. He knew Russia was starting to garrison it to threaten American interests once again. After all, Russia had already reclaimed its former Soviet satellites and was in the process of suppressing its former Warsaw Pact "allies." Reinvigorating Cuba as a threat to America was part of that return to Soviet times.

Keaven would be in Cuba, monitoring everything the Russians were doing, again secretly off the CIA's books. The years he spent on studying Spanish would now play a part in infiltrating Cuba.

As Keaven expected, the Russians had most assuredly begun garrisoning Cuba again. Now with renewed economic power from reacquiring vast resources from their conquests, the Russians began sending money to the Cubans to foment rebellion in the Western Hemisphere. Concomitantly, the Russians did begin placing special forces, naval, air force, intelligence, and other assets in Cuba.

In Havana's harbor in 2021 sat the Admiral Kuznetsov aircraft carrier, Admiral Nakimov battlecruiser, Moskva cruiser, Udaloy destroyer, Admiral Kharmalov destroyer, Admiral Isakov frigate, Steregushchiy corvette, Grayvoron corvette, Marshal Krylov missile-ranging ship, Vlad Putrin intelligence ship, Mikhail Gorbachev communications ship, K-550 Aleksandr Nevskiy submarine, K-186 Omsk submarine, K-335 Gepard submarine, and B-265 Krasnodar submarine. They were all part of the newly designated Western Hemisphere fleet with their port of call in Havana. Admiral Korolev was the commander of this naval presence.

At Havana's military airstrip were the following Russian planes: 10 Su-35S's (Flankers) multirole fighters and 10 MiG-29M's (Fulcrums) multirole fighters. Colonel General Viktor Bondarev was the commander of the air force presence.

There were also about 1,000 Russian Special Forces troops (Spetsnaz) as part of the 45th Guards Detached Spetsnaz Brigade. In addition, 100 agents as part of the SVR RF (new KGB) special forces were present (Zaslon). Ten military transport planes were deployed as part of this group to get these soldiers to anywhere in the world at any point in time.

Spetsnaz soldiers were considered to be the best in the world. Many died in the sorting out process of who was good enough to join.

The group's most renowned mission occurred during the Soviet-Afghan War. Operation Storm-333 resulted in the Spetsnaz assassinating Afghan President Hafizullah Amin. As part of the operation, his 200 personal guards were also killed.

The Soviets installed President Babrak Karmal in the aftermath. 660 Spetsnaz dressed in Afghani military uniforms with 50 now Zaslon intelligence officers executed the mission. Osama bin Laden had great respect for the Spetsnaz, believing their air-assault tactics to have changed the face of the war.

As if all that firepower 90 miles from Key West, a place Keaven knew well, were not menacing enough, Keaven was the first to discover four RS-24 Yars SS-29 intercontinental ballistic missiles on mobile trucks and two RT-2PM Topol SS-25 Sickle ICBMs on mobile trucks. They were well camouflaged. In fact, they took advantage of new camouflage technologies that used cameras to project the ground image toward the sky as if nothing were even there.

Six ICBMs would have six pre-programmed targets. Most likely, the targets would be San Francisco, Los Angeles, Houston, Chicago, DC, and NYC. The radioactive fallout from NYC would take out Philadelphia and Boston. 100 million American lives could be extinguished in seconds. In addition, the ICBMs on the subs that were seen and unseen would take out anybody left. The missile shield for the US was never designed to react quickly enough for a surprise ICBM launch from Cuba. Again, even if it were, all it would take is an electromagnetic strike to take out the missile defense shield. These missiles would then reach their targets.

As Keaven reported the steadily advancing garrisoning of Cuba, Matt could only react with shock. Nobody really believed the Russians would renege on the Cuban Missile Crisis agreement. However, they apparently had. Evidently, it was all part of Vlad Putrin's objective of revenge.

It was soon enough time for Keaven to make a decision. His decision was to run for the 2024 election cycle for President of the US by first securing the Republican nomination. He left Cuba in 2021.

23 2024 RUN

Keaven convinced the Republican National Committee to let him be part of the first debate

despite resentment at the damage he had caused Truism in the last nomination process. The resentment largely came from the large contingent of candidates connected to Truism now standing next to him. Facing him on the stage were Truism's Vice President; Truism's son, Neville Truism, Jr.; Truism's Secretary of State; Truism's Attorney General; and a noted former CEO, who just happened to be a woman, Rachel Dunning. The next Republican Presidential nominee would have some connection to Truism unless Keaven or Rachel beat the odds.

Keaven tried to tell God to stay out of it other than as an adviser. However, used to NSA work and long with his addiction, he kept hacking.

Optics usually matter more than words unfortunately. Thus, the debates passed without much differentiating among the candidates, nobody wanting to stand out yet.

Keaven decided that he had to do more this time around to generate positive publicity for his campaign. He began by challenging Magic Lansing to a game of "vote." It was "horse" but with a shorter name. Magic Lansing, though staying mostly away from politics, was a lynchpin for Keaven's idea of converting Democrats into Deal Republicans. Keaven had played enough in midnight basketball leagues to develop a great shot. Keaven also was wise. Magic was not necessarily known for his shooting touch despite being a Hall-of-

Fame inductee. Keaven assured that media were present because he knew he would win. Magic only agreed to it because he knew of how much charity work Keaven had done for his community.

Because he was not a basketball player by trade, Keaven asked for the right to start. As such, he controlled the battle. His first shot was a left-handed free throw. Magic missed. "V" for Magic was the starting battle cry.

Then Keaven ripped a right-handed free throw. Magic made it.

Keaven banked in a shot from the right elbow, calling bank. Magic missed. "VO" was then the score.

Keaven did a 360-degree slam dunk. The reporters' revealed their immense shock. Magic missed. "VOT" was now the score.

Finally, Keaven closed it out with a drive to the free throw line, 360-degree pivot, fall-away jumper. It was nothing but net. Magic somehow made it. Keaven repeated the move but this time with the left-handed shot. Magic missed. "VOTE" was the score, and the contest was over.

Magic thanked Keaven for his charitable work. Keaven thanked Magic for the opportunity.

At the end as the media interviewed Magic, he had these comments, "I've generally voted Democratic, but there's something about Keaven Deal. He has volunteered to help so many individuals over his lifetime. He's not the typical Republican. If I were voting in the Republican primary, I would vote for him. In a general election against a Democratic Presidential nominee, I don't know. It would be difficult on me. I have this final comment. After what I've just seen, don't bet against him becoming the next President of the US."

Jerome did Keaven a favor by using his connection to Canoe East, the rapper. Jerome arranged for a rap off. Of course, Canoe East had already endorsed whomever the Democratic nominee was as a better candidate than any Republican.

This time, there were stakes. If Keaven lost, he would have to wear a shirt, saying "Vote Democratic" for media photos. If Keaven won, Canoe would have to wear a shirt, saying "Vote Deal for President." The judges would be the crowd of young voters comprised of equal numbers of registered Republicans and registered Democrats.

God told him he had no chance of winning. However, Mo did not understand Keaven's insight into rap. Keaven virtually grew up in the streets of NYC as he attended UNIS. Rap was part of fitting in.

This time, Keaven wanted the last word, so he let Canoe start first. Canoe began with a strong backbeat provided by his DJ, "Republicans are vampires, taking from the poor and giving to the rich: Robin Hood in reverse. Time to switch it up. Time for taxing the rich even more to give to the poor. Time for the US to take care of its own before taking care of those overseas. Peace out."

It was now Keaven's turn. Mo was his DJ for the moment. All things involving tech were well within Mo's control. Mo provided the backbeat, and it was hypnotizing. He must have spent countless hours finding it, but somehow it was like magic. The words instantly came to mind as Mo played. Keaven began, "Democrats are vampires, taking from the poor, taking from the rich, ignoring the middle: Time for the middle class to matter. Time for you to keep your money instead of government telling you where it should be. Time to be free. Bury your heads in the sand, and peace will be out of the question."

Whether it was good rap or not, Keaven won. The crowd believed in the power of words, not the power of celebrity. Suddenly, the rest of the Republican establishment started to take notice. A middle-aged white man was convincing traditionally Democratic groups to join his cause. Keaven took a great picture with Canoe wearing a "Vote Deal for President" shirt.

Keaven had many slogans all the way from "The Real Deal" to "Heaven Votes Keaven" to "Keaven-Sent Deal" to "Deal of the Millennium" to "Seventh Keaven" to "The Real New Deal." Mo helped of course.

As for his California crew, Jessie, his stepbrother, took leave from his job as a police officer in Compton, California, to help Keaven campaign. Raul, his other stepbrother, went on to work for the FBI but took leave to help as well. Both were so moved by Keaven's speech regarding Rosa that they had pursued careers to help the public.

As for his intelligence community friends, Jerome had advanced rapidly in his career despite his former disability. Now, he was Assistant Director of the CIA. Matt had become the Director of National Intelligence. It was outside the CIA but in control of all intelligence for the US. Because of their positions, they could not take an active role in Keaven's campaign but shared information to the extent allowable to maintain Keaven's knowledge of world events.

Dana Denney now had a super church in Chicago, broadcasting her sermons nationwide. Matteo Martin had become the Director of the FAA. Colonel Cuba Libre was now in charge of the 33d Fighter Wing in Valparaiso, Florida. In 2009, he exchanged his F-15 for an F-35 Lightning II. Colonel Leatherneck had become the leader of the 919th Special Operations Wing, responsible for General Atomics MQ-1 Predator (drone) missions. He was also located in Florida.

As for his special forces friends, Terence, Sr., was in Charge of US Special Forces, United States Special Operations Command. Terence, Jr., was in charge of SEAL Team Six, moving from the Army to Navy based on his special qualifications. Again, they could not endorse a candidate, but they quietly shared with their comrades that a savior was on the way.

As for his UNIS friends, Shadia Selani had married a Jordanian royal and was now the First Lady of Jordan. Ehud Shamir was the leader of Israel. Marina Mikrob was the elected leader of Serbia despite Russian elements in her country. Andrija Horvati was the elected leader of Croatia also in spite of Russian elements also present in her country.

His UNIS friends recorded political ads for Keaven, saying essentially that, since they had known Keaven, he had always stood for peace. They mentioned that Keaven was the last and best hope for both freedom and peace in this world.

It was incredibly unusual for other countries' leaders to voice support for a particular candidate, especially so early in the election process. However, Keaven meant hope for them and the world in a time of darkness. They knew him and that he would stand up for what was right.

Surprisingly to Keaven, he started to pick up endorsements from places he did not even expect. Among the crowd gathered for his speech at Rosa's funeral was a future Academy Award winning actress, Elle Maclin, a person many considered to be the most beautiful woman in the world. She had remembered Keaven. Despite being a Democrat, she endorsed Keaven. She even cajoled her friends to lobby fellow actors and actresses to endorse Keaven.

Candidates from both parties became envious. Proving himself in these ways, money started to roll in for his PAC. He could finally afford television and internet ads. Thanks to ever-increasing support, he went on to become the Republican Presidential nominee.

A difficult decision was now at hand, whom to select as his running mate. The decision was made more difficult by the fact that Chel Bomban was the Democratic Presidential nominee. She was so charismatic and beloved and had an ace up her sleeve as the wife of former President Kanyay Bomban, who was ready to campaign for her. For her Vice President, she had selected Neville Truism's son, Markov Truism, seeking to gain Independent voters who had aligned themselves with Truism in his defeat of Hellon Colton. The ticket of a Bomban and a Truism would be difficult to defeat.

The Colton's were still around in the background, campaigning for Bomban-Truism to try to secure their own posts in the new administration. Unfortunately, it meant bitter reminders for Keaven of Chel Colton as she was now the front person for the Colton's.

As he debated his own Vice President selection with God and his stepbrothers, Keaven suddenly received a phone call. It was a former competitor who had pulled out of the nomination process long ago, Rachel Dunning.

She began, "Do you know who I am?"

Keaven responded, "Yes, I obviously know who you are by your voice, Ms. Dunning."

Rachel countered, "Please call me Rachel."

As kindly as he could, Keaven countered, "I'm kind of busy right now, so do you have a purpose behind this call?"

Rachel replied, "How about we meet for dinner tonight at 6:00 PM?"

Keaven looked at his cell phone time: 5:45 PM. He was in Miami, Florida, in advance of the Republican National Convention to begin in just days.

"If you're in LA with your husband right now, there's no way you'll get here in time," Keaven replied, laughing at the end.

Rachel responded with a more somber voice, "My husband and I have agreed to a divorce, so I am just a loyal Republican following you to Miami for the convention."

"I'm sorry. I didn't realize," Keaven countered as empathetically as he could.

"Some things were just meant to be . . . like you becoming President of the US," Rachel continued.

There was a knock on the door. Mo answered it, and Rachel was standing before them in an absolutely stunning gown. Keaven watched as Jessie's, Mo's, and Raul's mouths literally almost dropped to the floor. Keaven looked up simply with surprise. He commented, "The moment you said you were following me to Miami, I never expected you actually to be here."

"I'm here to support you all the way to the White House," Rachel commented.

Mo, regaining his senses, quickly said, "Good to see, you, Rachel, but we have important business to discuss, so . . . ."

Raul intervened, "We could all discuss the topic over dinner with Rachel."

Jessie cajoled, "Not a bad idea, my brother."

"Maybe next time, boys, but I've invited Keaven to a special night," Rachel interrupted.

Mo simply mentioned to Keaven, "Do you remember the moment I warned you about Chel?"

Keaven acknowledged Mo, saying, "Yes."

Mo continued, "Do you remember the price you paid for ignoring my advice?"

Keaven mentioned, "Yes."

Mo intoned, "Then listen carefully to what I will tell you now: We have important business, so Keaven will have to decline THE DATE with you."

Rachel countered, "You make old friends meeting seem so formal. Date? What is a date?"

Keaven replied, "I need all the supporters I can get, Mo. You know that."

Mo intervened, "Have we not been through this exact moment before and lived with the consequences for the rest of our lives so that, as Santayana said, we don't have to relive history?"

Keaven responded, "It's just a meeting."

Mo countered with rising anger, "It's always just a meeting, the type that ends up damaging your soul and the souls of everybody around you who cares about you."

"You can use the time to form your combined recommendation with Raul and Jessie. I trust you guys as much as I trust anybody in the world," Keaven continued. "You'll get the right answer, possibly an even better answer without me present."

Keaven walked out the door with Rachel arm in arm. Mo could only wince. Raul and Jessie could only look enviously on as the door closed behind the two power brokers.

Mo began, "I don't like it."

Raul countered, "She's the ideal Vice President."

Jessie continued, "I agree with my brother. We need a woman on the ticket to counter Chel Bomban."

Mo disagreed, "Truism beat Hellon Colton with a male Vice President. Why can't Keaven?"

Jessie intervened, "What is it with you being so controlling of Keaven?"

Raul countered, "Jessie, remember he's God after all."

Jessie went on, "Whether you are God or not, you have to let him make his own decisions at some point in his life. You know he has a right to free will."

Mo countered, "I just know this whole scenario will only end up in tragedy. Despite the lack of women in Keaven's life on a permanent basis or because of it, he's way too susceptible to their influence. He fell for Chel Colton after all. By comparison, it's so much easier for him to fall for Rachel. That relationship would complicate the campaign beyond what you can believe. A single male Presidential candidate and a newly single female Vice Presidential candidate is just asking for trouble. What about a possible sexual harassment suit? Indeed, Keaven would be considered to be her direct superior."

Raul replied, "You have to trust Keaven at some point in time."

Jessie continued, "The very fact that he is single all the more requires him to pick a woman as the Vice President. Otherwise, certain uncomfortable rumors could start to make the rounds."

Mo retorted, "Rumors can make the rounds whether he selects her or not. With all due respect guys, I know him better than you two do. I know how a woman can play with him."

Raul continued, "Even so, why do you continue to lack faith in him?"

Jessie countered, "The vote's two to one, Mo, in favor of her being the Vice President on the ticket.

Raul said for reassurance, "She has been a successful businesswoman, looks stunning in an evening gown, and could grow Keaven's following among women. Case closed."

Mo replied, "If Keaven votes no, it's two to two. Tie's to the side with Keaven voting for it."

Raul said, "Agreed."

Jessie then said, "All right."

Keaven and Rachel were now in the downstairs restaurant. Keaven began by saying, "I'm not really up to eating. I kind of have a routine of eating only twice a day a simple meal of bagels."

Rachel countered, "Are you kidding me? Democrats could use just that to illustrate to Americans that you're not normal."

Keaven replied, "I'm extraordinary, not normal. I'm a Reagan-Lincoln Republican in a land of Truism Republicans and Democrats."

"You don't know much about dating. Do you?" Rachel responded.

Keaven questioned, "I thought this meeting was anything but a date?"

"Working so many hours each day as a CEO teaches a person something," Rachel continued. "It educates you to see in every moment the amazing possibilities."

"You should know that my heart's already taken," Keaven continued.

"What do you mean?" Rachel questioned.

"My heart's reserved for Tricia until I see her again in Heaven," Keaven replied.

"Come on. You don't really believe in the religious rhetoric. Do you?" Rachel asked.

"What I say is what's in my heart. I'm not a liar. Everything I say, I believe in," Keaven countered.

"That's why you need me in your life," Rachel countered. "I can teach you about how the world really works."

"With all due respect, Rachel, I doubt you could even begin to understand how this world works," Keaven replied.

"Have you ever served as a CEO of a Fortune 500 company, one of the first women to do so?" Rachel countered. "You have no idea what it feels like constantly to be scrutinized and have to live up to some standard not just for yourself but for all women."

"While it may have seemed like a burden to you, I know millions if not billions of other citizens of this planet who would happily trade their situations for yours," Keaven countered.

Her anger rising, Rachel demanded, "What have you ever done?"

"The tale of my life is way too long and way too boring," Keaven remarked. He stood up to leave to finish his conversation with Mo and his stepbrothers.

Rachel cooled down, pleading, "Give me another shot. You're different than any other man I've ever met." Keaven decided to sit down again.

"Let's make this simple, Rachel," Keaven said. "What do you really want?"

"Isn't it obvious?" Rachel replied with a wry smile.

"No," Keaven responded.

"You," Rachel coyly countered.

"Let me help you with that. You want the person who wants to be

President. You want to be connected with the power. You don't want me," Keaven countered.

Rachel retorted, "I get what I want."

"Not this time," Keaven countered.

"So you don't like women?" Rachel countered.

"Have I not just told you my heart's reserved for Tricia?" Keaven questioned.

"All right. I'll take the bait. Who's Tricia, and why's she in Heaven?" Rachel politely demanded.

Keaven explained, "She was a dual-sport athlete at Berkeley, who wanted to marry me to become First Lady and loved me in spite of myself. She died in 9/11 before I could my Learjet and helicopter could reach her. She's the reason I spent two years in graduate school to satisfy the CIA I was sane enough to get to pursue her killer. I spent almost nine years in Pakistan and finally did get bin Laden for her."

"If you ever tell the press that tale, they'll show you're a liar," Rachel unsympathetically countered.

"Why are you calling me a liar?" Keaven demanded.

Rachel explained, "The FAA grounded all civilian aircraft, especially around NYC, in instants on 9/11, so you could have never been en route to her through the air. Given your graduate school degree requires an extra year beyond your time at Illinois, you could never have earned that particular degree. Finally, you did not catch bin Laden. You were never listed as part of Operation Neptune Spear or any of the accounts of that day. See. You're interested in me, just trying to impress me with tall tales."

Exasperated, Keaven disclosed, "Cuba Libre, Leatherneck, and Matteo Martin will vouch for my activities on 9/11. Dana Denney and Jerome will assure you of my graduate degree attainment. Finally, the current DNI, in private, would confirm that I worked for him as a CIA operative off the books. He would also confirm that I personally secured bin Laden before the SEAL team   arrived   by foiling a Russian intelligence evac of him and then knocking him unconscious during his escape attempt in advance of the attack."

Rachel continued, "Now can you see how powerful I can be? I have tales from you that no media outlet could get from you before."

Keaven sighed, saying, "God was right about you."

"Again with that religious stuff really?" Rachel asked.

Keaven replied, "Let's agree to disagree, so you don't want to be Vice President."

Rachel countered, "Do you see what I mean about being powerful? In negotiating, you always start by asking for more than you want. Then, as the other side backs down, you win."

Keaven questioned, "So in other words, you were never interested in me, in dating me, but were just using it as a bargaining tactic?"

Rachel said, "What did you think?"

Keaven sarcastically responded, "Rhetorical questions are great. Enjoy your time in Miami, Rachel."

"How about we go to a nightclub and dance? It's what you do in Miami," Rachel continued.

"Surprisingly, I have better things to do with my time. If you need a partner, I'm sure your ex-husband is available," Keaven finished. He walked away to meet Mo and his stepbrothers.

On returning, Keaven said, "You were right, Mo."

Mo then said, "Two to two now. I win."

Raul tried to cajole Keaven, "She's great eye candy. She's a great businesswoman. For all your service to the common person, you don't have much of a record of helping the business community."

Keaven ironically responded, "No, I just helped incorporate virtually every Fortune 500 and Global 2000 subsidiary set up in Pakistan for over ten years."

Jessie then began the campaign for Rachel as Vice President, "You need a woman on your ticket. You don't have any women in your life. It looks bad, really bad."

Mo countered, "Yes, optics are important, but Keaven is better without a distraction."

Keaven angrily retorted, "You don't have to continue to watch out for Tricia's interests, Mo. She's gone."

Mo replied, "We all know why she's gone."

Raul mentioned, "Cool it."

Jessie continued, "We have a tie. We'll have to find some way to resolve it."

Raul continued, "I mean. What other legitimate candidates are there for Vice President? She's the only one of your nominee contenders who's not related to Truism in some way."

Mo intoned, "We don't know that for sure given all Truism's liaisons."

Jessie countered, "Come on."

Keaven mentioned, "What about some of my friends in intelligence or in the military?"

Jessie intervened, "You're already tough enough to the public, maybe even too tough. They all remember Truism's sucker punch of you and you continuing in the debate. You don't need to prove you are a tough guy by including a military guy on the ticket."

Raul countered, "What do you have against her?"

Keaven revealed, "She's manipulative."

Jessie replied, "Who isn't in politics?"

Keaven countered, "I'm not."

Raul then said the magic words, "She could help win you California."

Mo countered, "Dream on. I lived in California for years. No Republican since Reagan has won it, and even that success could have been a fluke."

"If we win California, we win the election," Keaven responded.

Mo sarcastically mentioned, "If you want to win California, why not choose Chel Colton as your running mate?"

Jessie interrupted, "Back to reality here, guys. Whomever we select has to beat Markov Truism in a debate. Who can? That question could help us get some resolution here."

Mo questioned, "What about that gal who ran as Vice President for the Republican ticket a few times ago? She has to be better than Rachel. Right?"

Raul countered, "Are you kidding me? Rachel has the brains and the body."

Keaven intervened, "Who cares about her body?"

Jessie interrupted, "I do."

Keaven countered, "You and Raul are acting just like you used to be at Beverly Hills High School, not like who you really are now. We have to find a way to win. You can't win an election with a Vice Presidential pick, but you certainly can lose one with a poor choice."

Mo implored, "What about one of Reagan's kids? It would get everybody thinking about how you're a Reagan Republican."

Jessie replied, "There are very few of us who remember Reagan's administration, and a name is just a name. They don't carry any clout."

Keaven interjected, "I have a lot of respect for anybody with the last name of Reagan."

Raul jabbed, "What about one of the Bush brothers, Neil, Marvin, or . . . ?"

Keaven interrupted, "While I have great respect for each and every one of them, I don't think it's the right fit."

Mo implored, "One of the Bush's could get you all-important Florida."

Raul replied, "Keaven already has Florida for how many years he lived there."

Mo countered, "There are no guarantees, and somebody with connections there would help us, giving us credibility with the Republican establishment."

Jessie said, "The Bush's don't want to run."

"We haven't asked any of them yet," Mo continued.

There was another knock on the door. Mo replied, "Nobody's home."

Keaven remarked, "We have to answer it. We can't afford to lose anybody's vote."

It was the current RNC chairman. He began, "Have you decided on your Vice President pick?"

Mo answered, "We're currently debating it."

The RNC chairman mentioned, "I just talked with Rachel Dunning. She's stunning by the way, and I believe you need a woman on your ticket."

Mo replied, "Who has Rachel not seduced tonight?"

Raul countered, "We finally have a tiebreaker."

Mo continued, "It's Keaven's choice in the end."

Jessie asked, "What is it then, Keaven? Who's your pick?"

Keaven countered, "With a Truism on the Democrats' ticket, we can't take anybody attached with Truism. I wouldn't even if there weren't a Truism on the Democrats' ticket. That choice basically just leaves me with Rachel. While there are compelling choices for selecting her, we don't mesh well."

The RNC chairman intervened, "You don't have to live together. You each have your own separate residence. You need women to vote for you. Rumors will start if you don't begin associating yourself with some woman at least. There are worse women in the world. Come on. You're representing our party as well. We need women to turn out for us as a party in the general election."

Mo interjected for the last time, "Just remember, Tricia and Chel. Just remember this moment that God is warning you again that tragedy will come from this choice if wrongly made."

"I pray that I've made the right decision, agreeing to select Rachel Dunning as my Vice President," Keaven replied.

"Tricia and Rosa will roll over in their graves," Mo warned.

"Great," the RNC chairman shouted. "I'll run downstairs to tell Rachel."

Mo intervened, "Thank you for your willingness, but that news is for Keaven to share."

Mo then spoke directly to Keaven, "You made your bed, so let's see you lie down on it."

Keaven countered, "You don't have the metaphor quite correct, Mo."

Mo countered, "I meant it as I said it. It's your choice. Tell it to her face now, and don't bother me the next time tragedy strikes."

Raul and Jessie had smiles on their faces, their choice prevailing. They wanted Keaven to win and believed Rachel to be the ticket to the White House.

Keaven took the elevator to the restaurant with the RNC chairman in tow. Unfortunately, Rachel was not there anymore.

"What do we do now?" Keaven asked.

The RNC chairman replied, "I have her phone number. I call her for us."

"I won't ask why you have her phone number, but I will say that you should call her for me," Keaven responded. "I need to get some things in line before I offer her the post."

The RNC chairman talked to Rachel on the phone and discovered she was at BED on 929 Washington Avenue. He told Keaven, "She's at BED."

"God knows everything," Keaven replied. "I'm not sure the optics of that situation would be good."

The RNC chairman said, "I can tell her for you."

"The optics would not be any better for you either," Keaven replied. He grabbed a stocking cap out of his pocket, trying to cover so much of his face as he could. Soon, Keaven was hailing a cab as inconspicuously as he could on his way to BED.

Keaven asked the cabdriver, "What do you know about BED?"

The cabdriver replied, "It's the hottest club in town. You and your date sit on a king-sized bed instead of on chairs at a table. House music is the style. BED stands for Beverage, Entertainment, and Dining. Don't be surprised to see all Miami's celebrities there."

Surely enough, on entering, there was Rachel sitting alone on a king-sized bed. All Keaven could do is pull the stocking cap farther down his face. He always had the stocking cap just in case he ever had to breakdance again. However, Keaven doubted whether he could pull off that feat at his age. The bouncer asked him to remove the stocking cap according to nightclub rules. "Great," Keaven mused. "Haven't I been through a bad dream like this sometime before?"

Surprisingly, nobody turned to look at Keaven. Maybe Miami nightclub attendees did not follow American politics that much. At least Keaven could hope for that fact.

Finally reaching Rachel's table or really bed, Keaven said somewhat sheepishly, "Can I sit down?"

Rachel looked up to see him with surprise, "What are you doing here?"

Keaven quipped, "I've asked myself that question every ten seconds since I walked in here."

"Mr. Clean-cut finally is willing to party on the wild side?" Rachel teased. "All right then. Sit down." Keaven sat down on the bed.

"What is an ex-CEO doing in a place like this?" Keaven asked.

Rachel responded, "Bad pick-up line."

"I'm being honest," Keaven retorted.

"I'm single now. I want to live the life I never could on my way up the corporate chain still as a married woman," Rachel replied.

"Potential Vice Presidential candidates can't live like this," Keaven countered.

"Is that a threat or a promise?" Rachel countered. "Are you going to spank me if I don't behave?"

Keaven replied, "What's your deal, Rachel? Are you on drugs? Are you unbalanced? Are you bipolar? I need to know seriously so that I can make a decision."

Rachel countered, "I'm just trying to cope with my marriage dissolving. I'm just trying to feel wanted. You dealt me a heavy blow, showing no interest in me. I'm still trying to recover from that."

Keaven questioned, "You said you were not really that interested in me. It was just a bargaining tactic."

Rachel replied, "I have some pride. I was trying to cover the hurt at not being good enough for you."

"At this point, you have me completely confused," Keaven continued.

"Why don't you understand women?" Rachel countered.

"It's my turn to ask questions," Keaven intervened. "Are you a Republican?"

"Yes, my conscience and by voter registration," Rachel answered.

"So far, so good. Do you see how easy this conversation can be?" Keaven replied. "What core Republican values do you believe in, and what do you not believe in?"

"Why are you not married?" Rachel interrupted.

"Please answer the question," Keaven implored.

"You please answer my question," Rachel countered.

"I asked first," Keaven replied

"I asked better," Rachel responded.

Keaven started to remember very similar past conversations with other women, something he did not want to have to remember especially now.

"Fine. I'll answer your question if you promise to answer mine," Rachel coerced.

"I surrender," Keaven acknowledged.

"I believe in whatever the President who selects me as Vice President believes," Rachel responded. "I will follow his lead in sickness and in health until death do us part."

"Not amusing," Keaven countered. "Insufficient, too."

Rachel responded, "We both know the Vice President is supposed to echo the President's lead, not vary from it. We both know I can beat Markov Truism in the Vice Presidential debate. We both know you don't understand women. If you want to win, you need a woman around you to be able to understand them and therein win their votes. Besides, wouldn't be great to get America starting to call us the next Camelot like JFK and Jacqueline."

Keaven countered, "JFK was President, and Jacqueline was First Lady, which was an entirely different scenario than President Deal and Vice President Dunning."

"Are you offering me the post or not?" Rachel questioned.

"It's yours," Keaven relented.

Rachel kissed him. Keaven quickly looked around the room to assure no cell phones had recorded this event. Unfortunately, it appeared that everybody had captured that moment. How could Keaven ever explain this situation to the press?

"Why did you do that?" Keaven asked with exasperation.

"I wanted to do so ever since I saw you stand up to Neville Truism in the Republican primaries years ago. You have this power over people. You know," Rachel explained.

"The press will ruin me . . . us over this," Keaven replied.

"What?" Rachel said, kissing him again.

Keaven pulled away and put a blanket between Rachel and himself to prevent any recurrences. "You're my Vice Presidential candidate, not my wife or significant other. It's time we both started acting like that."

Rachel countered, "There are no rules in the Constitution against the President and Vice President falling in love. We're both single. We're just kissing. That's all. Now I can fully understand how much you need me. You're worse off than I ever thought you were."

Keaven questioned, "Why are you doing this to me?"

Rachel replied, "What's your problem?"

"I need to feel untouchable. I need to feel that nobody can get to me by getting to someone who matters to me," Keaven replied.

"Thanks for finally answering my question on why you're not married yet. I didn't forget about it and would have forced you to answer it before the night was over," Rachel countered.

"Can't we go somewhere more private to talk?" Keaven countered.

"What do you mean?" Rachel questioned.

"It would be bad to say the words I'd like you to come back to my hotel room, so instead I will ask for your phone number," Keaven replied.

"I'm good with either," Rachel replied.

"Phone number," Keaven ventured with his head lowered in exasperation.

She took out a pen and wrote it on his right hand. Keaven replied, "Are you kidding me? You're acting like you're 18."

"You're acting like you're dead," Rachel countered.

Keaven had enough of this treatment. Fire was in his eyes in that particular moment. He went up to the DJ and paid him $100 for the right to spin some songs for the next 30 minutes.

The DJ instantly recognized Keaven from his rap battle with Canoe East and would have let him spin for free. $100, though, would help him pay his rent for the month.

Because the DJ set-up had Ableton, it allowed Keaven to create new mash-ups and remixes live. That fact was of great benefit given that he had not already programmed his songs.

He began by mashing up "With or Without You" with "Dreams." He went on to remix "Live Like You're Loved" with a dance backbeat. He continued the remixing with "Stranded." Then he mashed up "Born in the USA" with "What a Wonderful World." His final selection was the backbeat Mo used for his rap battle with Canoe East, the lyrics to which he rapped again this night.

All the while, Rachel was dancing in the crowd, cheering Keaven on. She just seemed to act like a teenager, somehow inspiring Keaven to do the same. While his selected songs did seem old school, the way he mashed and remixed them made them brand new to the audience. As he surrendered the turntables back to the regular DJ, he received a round of applause even from the DJ himself.

Keaven did not realize it, but national and local news crews somehow had found their way into the club videotaping his DJ efforts. The club owner no doubt had tipped them off to get better publicity. Thankfully, Keaven had given his best efforts, remembering the techniques from what he had learned long ago in the clubs of NYC while attending UNIS.

Rachel kissed him again. The cameras were there to catch that reaction this time without any question. The optics would not be good. In fact, Keaven noticed Mo standing among the assembled throng now, disapproval fully visible on his face.

His campaign had always been unconventional. With all the media present, Keaven said to Rachel, "Why not?"

Rachel replied, "Great DJing, but what do you mean by why not?"

Keaven pulled her over toward the national media, all networks in attendance, and then announced his Vice President pick amid the din of house music.

Keaven said, "I'm here tonight to celebrate the selection of Rachel Dunning as my ticket's Vice Presidential candidate. We'll have further remarks during the course of the convention, but, for right now then, you can run with this news."

Rachel countered, "That was Coltonian."

Keaven replied, "That's insulting."

Rachel replied, "It's a tribute to your ability to adapt to the situation."

A member of the press asked, "Why did you announce in a nightclub? Are you trying to break your characterization as a member of the religious right?"

Keaven replied, "I heard from a good friend that, if you're in Miami, you're supposed to be at a nightclub. Who am I to argue with tradition?"

Another reporter asked, "Why are you trying so hard to relate with young voters?"

Keaven countered, "Because I'm young myself."

The reporter interjected, "You're . . . ."

"I'll finish the sentence for you: young enough to DJ, rap, breakdance, dunk, and win the Presidency of the United States," Keaven interrupted. "By the way here, Chel Bomban is older than I am, but I don't believe in calendar age. It's how you feel that counts. Right, Chel?"

Mo intervened, saying, "As Keaven said, there will be time for further questions later. This is a celebration."

Mo was trying to adapt, but Keaven knew he would have some stern words for him out of the reach of the media. For the time being, Keaven was dancing with Rachel in the midst of the crowd.

Raul and Jessie showed up, too.

24 THE FIRST PRESIDENTIAL DEBATE

Anderson Coolson was the debate moderator. He announced time for closing remarks. Soon it was Keaven's turn to speak: "We face a choice right now. Our economy and the world are at their darkest hour of this century. We can surrender, or we can work together to solve these tasks.

The difference between the Democrats and Republicans is simply this. A mountain is before us in domestic and in foreign policy. The Democrats say the mountain is immovable. Republicans instead say: Bring in the engineers to place charges to turn the mountain into a mole hill. Then requisition the bulldozers, shovels, and dump trucks to pick up the debris. One party surrenders. The other party finds a solution.

We are at our darkest hour because Ronald Reagan's lessons have been forgotten. He taught us that the Soviet leaders, now Russian leaders, were evil. How are we then surprised that, after our refusal to fulfill our treaty obligations, the Russian military reoccupied all their former Soviet satellites and rested control over their Warsaw Pact 'allies'? Why are we surprised that China took Taiwan with nary a shot being fired in defense? The Syrian War continues, every day threatening to evolve into full-scale conflict throughout the Middle East. Cuba has become the largest Russian military base in the world just ninety miles from the US. Russia has abrogated the agreement resolving the Cuban Missile Crisis and the START treaties regarding nuclear weapon reductions. While we produce no new nuclear ICBMs, they are producing hundreds each year.

It must make us ask why. Why would Russia need so many nuclear weapons? The uncomfortable answer is to overwhelm whatever missile defense strategy that we can implement. That way, they have power over the world to take country after country, improving their failing economy by expropriating from others, our friends to whom we failed to honor treaty mutual defense obligations. Our word is our bond. It must be enforced, or freedom and security are in peril.

Meanwhile, our economy is in tatters because the world economy is in tatters. Both are due in part to the fear of growing global conflict but also because of poor fiscal and monetary policies.

Our government continues to tax at way too high of rates. Our tax system is so complicated that a tenured professor of tax cannot even know every provision, so how then can the common citizen?

Our tax system is also so unfair, discriminating against immigrants based on their particular nationalities, discriminating against the poor for having to pay rent (not deductible) instead of mortgage interest (surely deductible), discriminating against the old by taxing social security benefits on too many occasions, and on and on.

Simultaneously, the government spends more than it takes in. This pattern jeopardizes the well-being of future generations and has allowed inflation to rise exponentially.

At the same time, jobs are found everywhere but in America. Citizens are so despondent at not being able to find a job that they leave the work force. Minority groups have been the most adversely affected in each circumstance.

For the sake of unity, we must de-emphasize finding differences among ourselves based on race, nationality, religion, and sex. Affirmative action programs should be based on economic status ultimately. Otherwise, they benefit the best of a class and do nothing for the rest, who have more obstacles to overcome. By de-emphasizing the racial part and instead emphasizing the economic status part, such programs can actually be of assistance.

A Republican President enacted affirmative action legislation after all. A Republican President saved an entire class of citizens from slavery. Why then should there be faith in a Democratic Party to save minorities? They've been unsuccessful in every regard.

Finally, the immigration dilemma must be resolved with more than a wall. Building the wall just led to undocumented immigrants coming to this country by sea, not by land. To solve the immigration dilemma for all time, we must increase the number of legal immigrants we accept through the immigration lottery each year. If we weight the number we take from each country based on the number of applicants from each country and say that anybody who comes to this country illegally will never be allowed in legally, we will in one fell swoop solve the problem for all time.

Last of all then and most important of all, we must respect religion. Our country was formed by those who sought religious freedom. Of all liberties, this liberty was the most prized. In the process of becoming more progressive, we somehow have lost our commitment to defending religion's place in this society. Our culture increasingly sees religion as an anachronism of a time where science could not explain all the mysteries of the universe.

The key difference between me and Chel, between Republicans and Democrats, is that I have plans to solve our mountainous problems. She has plans to spend time and money to find some solutions to them. I say case closed. I have solutions. We do not have time to wait for implementing those solutions. We must act before it's too late.

Dr. Joseph Warren's 'Boston Massacre Oration' provides us with the guiding words, 'Our country is in danger but not to be despaired of . . . . Our enemies are numerous and powerful, but . . . Heaven and earth will aid the resolution. On you [rely] the fortunes of America. You are to decide the important questions on which rest the happiness and the liberty of millions yet unborn. Act worthy of yourselves.'

I intend to do so. God, forever bless America. Thank you."

Afterward, Rachel hugged Keaven, congratulating him on winning the debate. Will, Hellon, and Chel Colton also went up to Keaven. They were not as congratulatory. In fact, Will took him to the side in the backstage area, saying, "What do you want to drop out of the election?"

Keaven replied, "Are you kidding me? Presidential candidates don't just drop out of elections."

Will mentioned, "Everybody has a skeleton in their closet."

Keaven countered, "I don't."

"Whether you do or don't doesn't matter," Will continued. "Skeletons can always be invented or fabricated."

"Everybody knows me so well by now that they'll be able to discern fabrications attached to me for what they are, fabrications," Keaven replied.

Will continued, "Everybody wants something."

"That's true," Keaven ironically said. "You seem to want to return to governing this country. The problem is that two terms are the maximum for service as President."

"I have an envelope with a wealthy benefactor's check for $10 million. Is that enough?" Will asked.

"I have more than enough money and am not for sale," Keaven replied with indignation.

"What post do you want in a Bomban administration?" Will questioned. "You can have what you want. How about Secretary of State then?"

"If I win the election, I'll be President of the US," Keaven replied. "Consequently, Secretary of State somehow is not enough."

"You know. I'm sick of putting up with you," Will continued.

"It's interesting. Everybody says the same thing about you," Keaven retorted.

"What if you just disappeared as if you never existed?" Will countered.

"If you're threatening my life, just know that I'm untouchable," Keaven answered. "For me, death is preferable to life. It gets me closer to the ones I love most in Heaven."

"If you're dead, you can't be elected President. Can you?" Will menacingly remarked.

"Besides, everybody knows you are touchable because of your relationship with Rachel," Will continued. "I don't blame you. She's one hot . . . ."

Keaven interrupted, "I know I'm winning because you wouldn't be offering anything or even talking to me if I weren't." He continued, "When was the first time you sold out, Will, the first time that pursuing women or money became more important than doing what was right for the country?"

Will Colton punched him, saying, "Sorry. I slipped and inadvertently extended my right arm to brace myself. Unfortunately, it connected with your face."

"Here's another cheek. Have another shot at pretending to fall and see whether you can hit me in that cheek, too?" Keaven replied.

Will's Secret Service detail stepped in to extricate him from the situation. Chel came to Keaven's side next, saying, "We had something once. Why don't we find a restaurant somewhere so that we can talk as friends?"

Keaven replied, "Been there. Done that. Not returning."

Suddenly, Rachel was at his side, brushing Chel away. Rachel said, "You're out of touch and out of time. Goodbye, Chel."

Rachel asked, "What happened to your face, Keaven?"

Keaven replied, "Don't worry about it. During my two runs for President, two former Presidents have punched me. The interesting thing is I've never felt better."

Rachel, now figuring out the situation, still had to laugh at the joke. She replied, "They just are getting scared because you're leading

Chel Bomban by 10 points and are projected to win more than enough electoral votes. They want back in government, but you're set to ensure they never return."

"It's a month before the election," Keaven remarked. "A lot can happen."

25 FINAL DEBATE

The day before the final debate, Keaven was walking with Mo, Rachel, Raul, Jessie, and his small four-person Secret Service detail toward the hall for the final debate. Keaven wanted less Secret Service than recommended because he wanted to be able to interact with crowds. He also wanted to look approachable.

Something seemed different with the detail, though. Keaven noticed little things in their gait. Suddenly, the four pulled guns on Keaven and his friends. Keaven guessed what was up. He told them in Russian to drop the guns, another language he had picked up over the years. They undoubtedly were part of the Zaslon unit from Cuba, trying to interfere with US politics.

As Keaven tried to negotiate with them, Raul and Jessie drew their service weapons. They took two of them out. Keaven knocked the weapons in one fell swoop from the remaining two. Facing Raul's and Jessie's guns, the two put their hands up in the air. Raul and Jessie handcuffed them and then knocked them out.

Just as everything seemed to be quieting down, two Dragunov sniper rifle bullets pierced the air. They hit Keaven in the left arm and the right chest. Keaven was knocked to the ground and bleeding profusely. Raul opened his first-aid kit that he carried with him. Jessie fired shots in the direction of the oncoming bullets. Mo sent a 911 message, requesting ambulances and police. He also notified counter-terrorism units to travel to the area. Rachel hovered over Keaven.

Mo then reached for Rachel's arm, dragging her to safety out of the line of fire. Mo knew that, no matter how much he wanted to watch over Keaven, for the country's protection, he had to ensure that Rachel would still be alive to run for President.

Jessie found a way to the top of the building from which the snipers fired. The two snipers had left their guns and made a successful escape. Jessie returned to Keaven, telling Raul, "They left their guns and disappeared."

Rachel then ran over toward Keaven, asking everybody, "What just happened?"

Mo plaintively remarked, "Evil just took out the savior of this world."

Raul replied, "Not yet. My brother's not going to die."

Mo then responded, "If he can be saved, then he can't be taken to some hospital everybody knows about. They'll never stop until he's dead."

Rachel asked, "What do you mean?"

Mo from his years of experience in intelligence and watching over Keaven knew very well what Keaven knew, "They were Zaslon, the best of Russian intelligence officers. Vlad Putrin's wanted Keaven dead for a long time."

The ambulance, police, and counter-terrorism units arrived. Raul climbed in the passenger side of the ambulance, tears starting to fall from his eyes, but still present to guard his brother. Jessie was in the back of the ambulance with Keaven, trying to wipe the tears away from his eyes. They both had felt they had let Keaven down once already this day and hoped not to let anybody get close enough to be able to hurt him again.

Mo drove Rachel back to their hotel, knowing she could well be in need of protection. Mo, after all, could watch over Keaven from anywhere in the world. He could not, though, help but feel insufficient on this day. He had watched over him so many years. How had he not done his job this day?

Mo contacted all Keaven's closest friends. Jerome was obviously busy at the moment implementing CIA protocols, trying to diagnose what could follow. Matt was consumed with the same task. Cuba Libre was in the midst of a fighter-jet scramble as the US had been placed on DEFCON 4 in response to the attack on Keaven. Leatherneck was overseeing drone reconnaissance of Cuba.

Dana Denney flew to Dallas to be with Keaven. Terence, Sr., was activating USSOC resources. Terence, Jr., was put on ready notice for SEAL intervention.

The emergency room doctor told Raul and Jessie to leave Keaven's side. They would not, so he finally relented and told them to put on scrubs.

He said, "I can't guarantee he'll survive."

As they cut threw his suit, though, the doctor said, "Oh, my gosh." He showed Raul and Jessie Darren's Medal of Honor that Keaven had in his right shirt pocket. It was smashed almost to bits, but it had withstood most of the bullet's impact. Unfortunately, though, the bullet had pierced Keaven's lung just enough anyway to cause extensive bleeding. The doctor said, "We could save him yet."

Suddenly, an attendant in the room pulled out a knife and stabbed Keaven in the chest on the operating table. Raul drew his firearm and fired accurately. Jessie yelled, "Everybody out of the operating room except the surgeon."

The doctor responded, "I need at least one person for anesthesia and one person to help hand me scalpels, etc."

"You have us two," Jessie responded.

Raul continued, "We'll have to trust you, but nobody else is coming in here."

The doctor countered, "I don't know if I can save him now. At best, I'll try to stop the bleeding, but he'll be in a coma for days. He may never wake up."

Jessie replied, "Do your job, Doctor."

After hours of surgery, the doctor indicated, "We're done. He's in a drug-induced coma now. I don't know if he'll ever awake from it."

Jessie and Raul ran into Dana, who was praying outside the surgery room. Dana asked, "How is he?"

Jessie replied, "Who are you?"

Dana countered, "I went to school with his mom at Liberty University. I helped him through a tough time in his life."

Raul pushed Jessie to the side, saying, "I've seen her on television. She's a pastor, exactly what Keaven needs right now."

"Is he that bad?" Dana questioned with concern.

Jessie gravely answered, "Yes."

Despite the necessity of ensuring continuity of leadership of some sorts, Mo had relented to Rachel's demands. In that moment, the two of them walked into the waiting room where Dana, Jessie, and Raul were gathered.

Mo asked, "What's up?"

Raul answered, "Drug-induced coma from which he may never awake."

Rachel started crying. Dana gave her a hug. Mo was tearing up some, too. Mo replied, "What can we do?"

Raul said, "We have to get him to a secret location like you recommended."

Mo echoed the comment, "With Zaslon after him, he's not safe unless he's hidden."

Jessie countered, "Where can you possibly hide a Presidential candidate who is not yet President?"

Dana replied, "MacDill."

Terence, Jr. came in at that moment with Jerome. Terence, Jr., stated, "Right answer."

Rachel knew about Jr. and Jerome from long talks with Keaven. "You're at MacDill right? SEAL Team Six, too?"

Jerome answered, "Matt sent me. He can man the fort but wanted an intel op at Keaven's side, and, yes, Cuba Libre's and Leatherneck's units are in bound to give us transport and air support all the way there."

Mo cautioned, "The only problem with MacDill is it's closer to Cuba."

Jerome replied, "I know about the Russian garrison there."

Mo replied, "Only the Democrats don't seem to know or care about that fact. All these attackers are undoubtedly emanating from there."

Terence, Jr., countered, "If you can't trust special forces, you can't trust anybody. Besides, Cuba Libre and Leatherneck are stationed in Florida. We all now know each other through Keaven connecting us. In a time where trust is in doubt, connect with whom you know."

Mo relented, "All right."

Soon they were at MacDill in the base hospital. Dana, Raul, Jessie, Jerome, Rachel, and Mo were the only individuals allowed around Keaven other than trusted medical personnel. They were now Keaven's human shield. Terence, Jr., had his entire SEAL Team Six stationed around the hospital. Cuba Libre had two F-35 Lightning II's on combat air patrol over MacDill. Leatherneck had Predators gathering data over Havana to spot any movements toward the US shore. All knew what Keaven meant to this world, and all were prepared to pay the ultimate price to protect him.

Rachel was constantly in tears. Dana, Raul, Jessie, Jerome, and Mo tried to occupy her thoughts by telling her all that Keaven had accomplished in his lifetime.

Rachel replied, "How can one man accomplish all that?"

Mo responded, "All things are possible through God."

Dana echoed, "He's right, but Keaven has so much more to accomplish."

Mo intervened, "Rachel, you know that the debate is hours away. It's Sunday. Tonight is the final debate in Dallas. The national election is this Tuesday. You're going to have to get to Dallas and speak for Keaven. In fact, you'll have to speak as if you were now the Republican candidate for President. That means you'll have to start preparing with me as we climb aboard a passenger plane for Dallas."

Rachel countered, "How can I leave Keaven? He's the Presidential candidate, not me. How can they possibly still have the debate?"

Mo replied, "It's important to show that you are qualified. We have faith that Keaven will come back to us. However, you have to convince the voters of our faith in that outcome and simultaneously show that you would be competent to fulfil the role should Keaven not be."

Raul reassured her, "Keaven couldn't be in a safer place right now. You owe it to him to stand up for him tonight."

Jessie commanded, "You'll be great. There's a reason Raul and I wanted to pick you. You're the closest living thing to a Keaven Deal right now."

Dana replied, "I'll be praying for both of you."

Mo and Rachel began the flight back to Dallas. Mo began, "We should have known not to agree to a debate in Dallas. JFK's assassination."

Rachel countered, "Keaven's not dead yet, but I may be. I have nothing to say. Somehow, a Presidential election seems meaningless at this moment."

Mo questioned, "Don't tell me that you've fallen in love with him, too."

"What if I have?" Rachel demanded.

Mo responded, "Whether you know it or not, Rachel, every woman who falls for him experiences tragedy."

Rachel replied, "Small price to pay for being around a man who has accomplished all that I just heard, so what am I supposed to do tonight?"

Mo indicated, "I have contacted the debate host, asking if we could just do statements instead of a point-by-point debate given the situation. They've permitted us to alter the format in that way. We should thank Chel Bomban for being compassionate enough to agree to the changes."

Rachel intoned, "Of course she did for political reasons. She doesn't want to look like an ogre, attacking our side while everybody grieves for our leader. It would look pretty bad politically."

Mo replied, "I suppose."

"What do I say, Mo, God, or whatever your name is?" Rachel questioned.

Mo mentioned, "Tell the voters what you learned today and in your long conversations with Keaven, the tales they don't already know. Tell them about a man willing to spend almost a decade away from his country to fulfill a promise to his deceased wife-to-be. Tell them about a man who saved Cuba Libre from drowning, committed his life to others after failing Rosa, helped Jessie and Raul see the light, made Jerome a productive member of society, and on and on."

Rachel replied, "They'll never believe me. His tales are mythical, not real."

Mo responded, "I'll help. I have video of Keaven knocking bin Laden out to prove he really was there and important to that mission. I have video of the attack on him, the voters deserve to see those images as well. You convey the words and have faith in them. I'll convey the images."

Rachel did everything Mo said. Mo did everything he said. The nation now had a full picture of who Keaven was. Those citizens who believed in prayer then prayed for him. Those citizens who did not joined together in thinking positive thoughts regarding his recovery. America was moved by Rachel's words and Mo's images.

Keaven was still in a drug-induced coma. Rachel and Mo returned to his side after the debate. Whether Keaven was dreaming or his soul was somewhere else, Keaven started to see Heaven. Not only could he see Tricia, Rosa, his mom, and his dad, but Keaven could speak with them. In Heaven, he did not feel any pain, physical or even emotional. All those pains of his life were over. Keaven kept hugging Tricia, Rosa, his mom, and his dad over and over.

All the suffering was finally at an end. He had reached his ultimate goal, being with those he had loved once again. Joy like none he had ever experienced was inside him. Soon he was alone with Tricia, saying, "Will you marry me?" Although equally joyful in the moment, she said, "Your time on earth can't end now."

Keaven questioned, "What do you mean? I'm finally in Heaven with you. I fulfilled all the commitments I had on earth and went through hell on earth to do so."

"You know in your heart that you have so much more to accomplish," Tricia countered.

Keaven responded, "Don't you know how much I've dreamed of this very moment over the years? It kept me alive in Pakistan. I would look up at moonless skies in the midst of darkness surrounded by enemies, wondering how soon I would be able to see you again. It's the only thing that delivered me through the despair."

Tricia imparted, "You know that it was more than my memory that carried you through. God carried you through."

Keaven replied, "Why do you always have to talk about Mo?"

"By now, you know better than that. Don't you?" Tricia remarked.

"Isn't it God's turn to take care of the problems on earth?" Keaven demanded.

"Every life has a purpose," Tricia continued. "You know you were meant for more."

Keaven replied, "You don't know what you're asking of me. I can't live any longer without you."

Tricia interjected, "You know that Rachel loves you."

"That's meaningless," Keaven countered. "You know that you're the only woman I can ever really love."

Tricia replied, "It's not meaningless to her."

Keaven replied, "She'll live."

Tricia continued, "What about all the children suffering down there? Are they meaningless, too?"

Keaven countered, "I'm not God."

Tricia replied, "To them, you are the closest thing to God. You're hope in a time of darkness. You're safety in a sea of danger. You're life in the valley of death. How can you turn your back on them?"

"I could've found a way to get here sooner, but I fulfilled my obligations first. Please do not ask any more of me," Keaven pleaded.

Keaven suddenly had an image forming in his mind. The image

was of a little girl on her knees, praying. She was saying, "I don't know how to pray, God, but please hear what I'm saying. Please make Keaven well. Many bad things are happening to me right now. Somehow I know, though, that, if you can just get Keaven well, he'll come save me."

Keaven questioned, "Why are you doing this to me? Haven't I always done what was asked of me, going beyond what I thought was possible?"

Tricia commented, "You were never alone. You never did any of those great things on your own."

Keaven said, "Goodbye, Tricia. I can only hope and pray that I have the chance to see you again." He hugged her and then turned toward the image of the little girl. As he tried to walk toward her, Keaven began feeling pain beyond what he had ever felt. He wanted to give up. He did not know whether he could handle any more, but he kept walking. The pain kept increasing, but he was getting closer and closer to the girl. Because of the progress, Keaven was not planning on stopping.

Suddenly, he was surrounded by light. In front of his eyes now were Dana, Jessie, Raul, Jerome, Rachel, and Mo. Keaven wondered if this image was just another part of Heaven. Somehow with the amount of pain he was filling, he figured out that it was earth, not Heaven.

Rachel had his left hand in her right hand. Dana was holding his right hand in her left hand. Rachel said, "It's a miracle. He's awake."

Dana replied, "Thank you, God."

Keaven asked, "Where's the little girl?"

Raul questioned, "What little girl?"

Keaven replied, "I kept walking back from Heaven, trying to find a little girl who was praying for my help. I was getting closer and closer but suddenly found myself here surrounded by you."

Keaven tried to rise out of bed. Jessie and Jerome pushed him back down. Jessie said, "You have to rest."

"While there's a little girl out there somewhere suffering, I can't be lying in bed," Keaven commanded. "I have to find her and save her."

Mo asked the doctor now present, "Is he having hallucinations from the drugs you've given him?"

The doctor responded, "It's possible."

Rachel questioned, "Is there really a Heaven Keaven?"

Mo intervened, "Come on, Rachel."

"It seemed real enough to me," Keaven replied. "Tricia told me that you really love me."

Rachel replied, "Of course I do." She gripped Keaven's hand with a little more strength.

Dana intervened, "For somebody called God, Mo, it's surprising you have so little faith."

Keaven replied, "Don't get Dana started, Mo. She'll convert you or kill you in the process."

Mo remarked, "If you want to win the election, you have to get in front a television camera to show proof of life."

"How about skype?" Keaven replied.

"Works for me," Mo said, turning on his ever-present laptop with its own camera.

Mo replied, "All you have to do is show you're alive and are recovering."

Keaven demanded, "Get me a suit."

Raul countered, "Are you kidding?"

Keaven continued, "If Franklin Roosevelt can stand despite being confined to a wheelchair, I can stand. I can also wear a suit, too."

Rachel handed him his suit. She'd brought it with her as a good-luck charm. She remarked, "Always prepare for the best outcome, and it will happen."

Soon Keaven had a suit on over his medical gown. With Dana, Raul, Jessie, Jerome, Rachel, and Mo supporting him, Keaven stood up and faced the camera. Mo clicked a button, putting then on live feed that would be recorded and picked up by all the media in the world.

Keaven knew what to say, "Nobody ever told me running for President was going to be this hazardous to my health. I've been punched twice, shot twice, and quite possibly stabbed twice. I lost count because I was unconscious. You know what, though: I've never felt better. Why? Because the world has taken its best shot at me and I'm still standing.

I'm here today because somewhere there's a kid hurting who needs my help. Whether I'm President or not, I intend to save that kid. A President cares about every life, every American. Until all are free from suffering, I can't be free from suffering. Until then, none of us is free.

Tomorrow, as you vote for President, I ask you to vote what you know is right, not left, not right, but what is right. For those who pray, ask God's guidance. For those who don't, vote what's in your heart. If you do just that, whatever happens will be the right result.

I close these remarks, perhaps the last I ever give to you as a Presidential candidate, by saying what have now become common words for me. As Dr. Joseph Warren's 'Boston Massacre Oration' told us, 'Our country is in danger but not to be despaired of . . . . Our enemies are numerous and powerful, but . . . Heaven and earth will aid the resolution. On you [rely] the fortunes of America. You are to decide the important questions on which rest the happiness and the liberty of millions yet unborn. Act worthy of yourselves.'

I intend to do so. God, forever bless America. Thank you."

Voters used prayers and hearts as their guides, electing Keaven President of the United States. He won every state and garnered 70 percent of the popular vote. As landslides went, this election was the biggest ever despite the immense popularity of the other Presidential candidate.

Keaven spoke to what every American believed in and represented what was best about America. Many battles were still in front of him, but, with the help of God, Vice President Dunning, FBI Director Raul, Secretary of Defense Jessie, CIA Director Jerome, DNI Matt, Director of the Joint Chiefs of Staff Terence, Sr., and some other well-placed friends, Keaven was ready to save that child who needed help, America, and the world from darkness.

POSTSCRIPT

Does Keaven Deal exist? Yes, his spirit is inside each one of us. We always have a choice about whether we allow this spirit to rise or to fall.

There is also a real Keaven Deal, an average person of faith who loves his country. If his country ever needs him, Keaven Deal stands ready to serve.

The only question is whether Americans will recognize him. Will we let our eyes deceive, saying he does not look like a President? Will we let our ears confuse, saying he does not sound like a President?

Instead, will we listen with our souls and hearts for his coming? If we do, we will recognize Keaven Deal for what he represents, a chance for faith, unity, and peace to rise again.

ABOUT THE AUTHOR

J Loving has a series in the works, featuring the lead character, Keaven Deal. Can President Deal heal the nation and lead it and the world through the darkness? What happens to the relationship between Vice President Dunning and President Deal? Many tales are yet to be told.

www.ingramcontent.com/pod-product-compliance
Lightning Source LLC
Chambersburg PA
CBHW060243290526
45789CB00001B/170